Reading Rainbow Guide to Children's Books

The 101 Best Titles

by Twila C. Liggett, Ph.D. **BOOKSALE**
and Cynthia Mayer Benfield

With an introduction by LeVar Burton

A CITADEL PRESS BOOK
Published by Carol Publishing Group

A Citadel Press Book
Published by Carol Publishing Group
Citadel Press is a registered trademark of Carol Communications, Inc.
Editorial Offices: 600 Madison Avenue, New York, N.Y. 10022
Sales and Distribution Offices: 120 Enterprise Avenue, Secaucus, N.J. 07094
In Canada: Canadian Manda Group, P.O. Box 920, Station U, Toronto, Ontario M8Z 5P9
Queries regarding rights and permissions should be addressed to Carol Publishing Group,
600 Madison Avenue, New York, N.Y. 10022

Carol Publishing Group books are available at special discounts for bulk purchases, sales
promotion, fund-raising, or educational purposes. Special editions can be created to specifi-
cations. For details, contact Special Sales Department, Carol Publishing Group,
120 Enterprise Avenue, Secaucus, N.J. 07094

READING RAINBOW is a registered trademark of GPN/NETV LINCOLN and WNED-TV/
WNYPBA BUFFALO, All Rights Reserved. READING RAINBOW is a production of
GPN/NEBRASKA ETV NETWORK and WNED-TV, BUFFALO and is produced by
LANCIT MEDIA PRODUCTIONS, LTD., New York. Funding for READING RAINBOW is
provided by the KELLOGG COMPANY, THE CORPORATION FOR PUBLIC BROAD-
CASTING, THE NATIONAL SCIENCE FOUNDATION, THE PEW CHARITABLE
TRUSTS, THE ARTHUR VINING DAVIS FOUNDATIONS, and Public Television Viewers.

Reading Rainbow is exclusively licensed by Troma Licensing.

Manufactured in the United States of America
10 9 8 7 6 5 4 3 2 1

Library of Congress Cataloging-in-Publication Data

Liggett, Twila Christensen.
The Reading Rainbow guide to children's books : the 101 best titles / by Twila C. Liggett and
Cynthia Mayer Benfield : with an introd. by LeVar Burton.
    p.   cm.
"A Citadel Press book."
ISBN 1-55972-222-3
ISBN 0-8065-1493-0 (pbk.)
    1. Children's literature—Bibliography.   2. Children—United States—Books and reading.
3. Reading Rainbow.   I. Benfield, Cynthia Mayer.   II. Reading Rainbow.   III. Title.
Z1037.L7145   1994
[PN1009.A1]
028.1'62—dc20
93-46695
CIP

To my sister, Judy Christensen Davis, for her unconditional love and support.

Twila Christensen Liggett

With love to O.P.B. and EPG

Cynthia Mayer Benfield

Acknowledgments

I'd like to thank Cynthia Mayer Benfield for sharing her insightful view of children's literature with us and for the use of a previously written article about how we choose our books. I'd also like to thank Ellen Doherty for her spritely summaries of the 70+ Reading Rainbow episodes, and Lori Robinson and Martin Quinn for their creative use of word-processing programs. A special thanks goes to Jeff Sass for his vision of extending Reading Rainbow into the arena of quality licensing.

TWILA C. LIGGETT, PH.D.

I would like to thank Dr. Twila Liggett for the opportunity to introduce in these pages a tasting of the very best books. I would also like to thank Barbara Elleman, editor of *Book Links* magazine, at American Library Association, for sharing her endless knowledge in this field during our every conversation. Finally, thanks go to Carol Publishing Group and Editorial Director Hillel Black for publishing this important guide for readers of all ages.

CYNTHIA MAYER BENFIELD

Contents

Family

Music

Physically Challenged

Poetry and Verse

Science and Nature

Introduction

by LeVar Burton

The goal of *Reading Rainbow* has always been a simple one: to use the medium of television to bring children back to the world of literature and the magic of the written word.

When we first embarked on this journey over ten years ago, there was quite a bit of support for the claim that television was, in fact, the evil enemy of literature. There were those who said that television discouraged children from reading. I have never been of the opinion that television and books need to be banished to mutually exclusive worlds. Rather, I strongly believe that television can be an incredibly powerful tool for our own education and enlightenment.

For the makers of *Reading Rainbow*, it has been our most fervent desire to help create generations of passionate, literate human beings. Judging from the response we continually receive from teachers, parents, and our most important critics, children, I daresay we have achieved great success in this area. I am proud to be a part of *Reading Rainbow*, and helping kids discover new horizons through books. By using this guide, you too can encourage the children in your life to read for pleasure.

Why is reading for pleasure so important? First, children who read on their own generally do better in school. It's that simple. I've talked to many successful adults who are living proof. Because they acquired the habit of reading at an early age, they soon learned to love to read and open themselves up to new subjects or ideas, which made learning easier for them.

Reading for pleasure is as valuable as studying for a class or doing homework. It's all about expanding the mind and exercising that muscle called "imagination."

I was lucky as a child. I grew up in a family where reading was like breathing. Reading was expected in our home. My mother, an English teacher, in her leisure time was always reading a book. She set a great example, one that has stayed with me my whole life.

I have learned in my lifelong relationship with literature that, as a reader, the possibilities for discovery are endless. This is especially true for young people. Books can open up new worlds for kids. Books can spark their imagination. Books give them the stuff for their dreams. Best of all, books can provide children with a sense of what's possible in life, encouraging them to think, "Yes, I can do that!" or "I can be that too!"

I can't stress enough how important it is for you to play a role in encouraging your children to read. That's what this guide is all about. It can help you choose the kinds of books that will interest your youngsters, and because these books have appeared on *Reading Rainbow*, they are kid-tested and kid-approved.

Once you've selected a few titles, you can find them either at a bookstore or at one of my favorite places, the library. For hungry readers like me, there is no place better than the stacks at the local library.

The most important thing you can do—and also the simplest—is read to your children. If, like me, you grew up in a house where there was always someone to read to you before bedtime, you will understand the special feeling of hearing your favorite story read aloud. If you didn't, it's not too late to start now with your own kids. By sharing your time and your interest in reading with them, you will send them the message that reading is an important part of your life. You will give your children a gift they will treasure forever.

By bringing reading into your family's life, especially through some of the wonderful books listed in this guide, you will be creating an immeasurable bond with your children, and a joy that words cannot possibly describe.

Enjoy!

Behind the Scenes
at Reading Rainbow

by Twila C. Liggett

When did *Reading Rainbow* begin?

In 1980 Dr. Twila C. Liggett of GPN/Nebraska ETV Network in Lincoln, Nebraska, and Tony Buttino of WNED-TV in Buffalo, New York, teamed up with Cecily Truett and Larry Lancit of Lancit Media Productions, Ltd., New York City, to develop the *Reading Rainbow* concept. It took almost eighteen months of proposal making and fund-raising before the initial pilot program funding was awarded by the Kellogg Company and the Corporation for Public Broadcasting. That program, "Gila Monsters Meet You at the Airport," tested very successfully and, with just a small amount of fine tuning, became part of the first fifteen *Reading Rainbow* programs that aired in July 1983.

Why and how was LeVar Burton chosen?

From the beginning, we knew that we wanted a host who loved reading and would be a positive role model. Additionally, we thought that a male host would send a strong, very positive message about books to boys, who don't seem to fall in love with reading as readily as girls and who are frequently surrounded more often by literate women (teachers, mothers) than men who read.

The list of candidates kept growing, but the creative team did not feel that the right person had been identified. Serendipitously, Cecily Truett and Larry Lancit saw LeVar on a talk show and, impressed with his eloquence and intelligence, recommended him as host. Lacking audition funds in the budget, we were fortunately able to review previous public television programs featuring LeVar as a host/presenter. We were unanimous in our delight with his ability to project the personable warmth that has become his hallmark as host of *Reading Rainbow*. Once we experienced LeVar's on-screen charisma, there was no other candidate.

Luckily for us, LeVar's manager (a former English teacher) was intrigued with the premise of the series (we had not yet shot the pilot). She in turn spoke to LeVar, who thought that using television to get kids to read was a challenging project and signed on immediately for the pilot.

Not only was LeVar Burton a good choice, he has become our child viewers' best friend, teacher, and confidant. Children write to ask LeVar to go camping, come stay overnight (he can have the top bunk), or come to dinner. They believe that they have traveled with him to most of the locations and believe implicitly what he says. LeVar's endorsement and promotion of the love of reading and positive thinking on *Reading Rainbow* has made literacy become an achievable goal for millions of children.

What does a typical program look like?

Each *Reading Rainbow* program begins with a featured children's picture book, which is often narrated by a celebrity such as Bill Cosby, Ruby Dee, Jason Robards, Lola Falana, or Dixie Carter as the illustrations come alive on-screen.

Based on the theme of the book, the program then uses on-location segments to demonstrate that reading can literally take you anywhere. For example, the theme of *Hill of Fire* was extended by footage shot in Hawaii as Mount Kilauea erupted with glorious fury. Other locations have included a coral reef in the Florida Keys; the Library of Congress and the Vietnam Memorial in Washington, D.C.; the Sonoran Desert in Arizona; Montserrat in the West Indies; the Taos Pueblo in Taos, New Mexico; and many other exciting places. Depending upon its theme or design, an individual program may also include animation, music videos, dances, songs, or "kid on the street" interviews.

Finally, each program closes with several children who give enthusiastic and sometimes funny reviews of three additional books that reflect that episode's theme.

How are books selected for *Reading Rainbow*?

There are three categories of books on *Reading Rainbow. Feature books* are fully adapted and are the focal point of each program. For each feature book, there are three *review books*, titles that support the theme of the feature book and are reviewed on-camera by children. Occasionally, we use *highlight books*, titles whose subject matter is related to the focus of a program, but which may be too difficult for our audience of children to read without the help of an older sibling, parent, or friend.

We find books through recommendations by our viewers, with the advice of professionals in both childhood education and children's literature, and by looking everywhere and reading everything we can. We have a special interest in good stories featuring protagonists who represent a cross-section of cultures—African-American, Hispanic, Asian, and Native American. We also search for stories with female protagonists in positive and active roles.

As we read books, the qualities we look for in *Reading Rainbow* titles are (1) literary merit, (2) visual impact and artistic achievement, (3) adaptability to the television format, and (4) ability to interest children.

We consider a number of factors in determining literary merit. Awards and other acknowledgments of literary achievement are important to us. Not only new titles, but books that have stood the test of time, interest us. We look for diverse literary styles. A book must be appealing as a read-aloud. *Reading Rainbow* books must show viewers that reading can be a pleasurable and rewarding experience.

We are also interested in awards and other distinctions given to picture books in evaluating a title for visual impact and artistic achievement. Books with strong, vivid, colorful graphics and artistic humor are often selected as feature books.

"Adaptability" refers to the way the book will translate from print to television. There must be a strong relationship between story and art, and the art must be graphically suited to television.

Stories with too much graphic detail may get lost, as may those with too little. On television, action in picture books works better than atmosphere or mood. Occasionally we ask the original illustrator to color a black-and-white book to enhance the impact of the art.

Books meeting our criteria are tested with children. *Reading Rainbow* researchers visit schools in New York and suburban areas and read stories to groups of beginning readers who represent a range of cultures and socioeconomic levels. Questions are asked to determine children's reactions, opinions, and recall of the story. The story session is considered one of the most vital aspects of the selection process. If children don't respond enthusiastically to a book, it isn't used.

With the list narrowed down, proposed titles are sent to education and literary consultants. In-house we discuss each book's potential for a *Reading Rainbow* show. We agonize over decisions, make them, and contact the publishers for permission to use the books in the series. *Reading Rainbow* books must be available in bookstores and libraries nationwide, and publishers must go back to print if necessary to meet consumer demand. Publishers are also encouraged to put *Reading Rainbow* books into paperback, and many do.

We now have approximately 410 titles included in the *Reading Rainbow* booklist (see the Appendix for the complete list). Each book has been through the process of evaluating, testing, brainstorming, and adapting, and has finally reached our viewers. Over the ten years that *Reading Rainbow* has been on PBS, librarians, booksellers, parents, and teachers have reported a stunning increase in requests for books seen on the show. Sales of these books have dramatically increased, with some jumping as high as 900 percent. This impact has convinced the children's book and television community that *Reading Rainbow* is successful in motivating children to seek out good books.

How are narrators chosen for the books?

The process of choosing a narrator for *Reading Rainbow* begins with the book's characteristics. *Reading Rainbow* books cover a wide variety of subject matter and cultures. Therefore, matching the voice to the book makes the job a unique one.

The book content dictates every aspect of the talent selected. Who is the main character? What is their sex, age, and race? Humorous books may require a wacky voice (as in Phyllis Diller reading *Ludlow Laughs*) to grasp the feel and comedic quality of the book. In other instances, dramatic or "big" voices are necessary (as in James Earl Jones reading *Bringing the Rain to Kapiti Plain*).

Magical things frequently happen in the sound booth as performers bring their distinctive personalities to the reading. James Earl Jones originally took a lighthearted approach to his narration. However, once he thought about it and realized what an important message both the show and the book had, he called the producer and asked to do the reading again, this time giving a more serious and profound reading.

Peter Falk, who read *The Robbery at the Diamond Dog Diner*, was so committed to his role of a chicken that during a brief pause as the audio tape was being changed, he continued squawking and flapping his "wings" around the studio to maintain character.

Over the years, *Reading Rainbow* has had the opportunity to work with an illustrious group of actors, including Edward Asner, Jason Robards, Madeline Kahn, Martin Short, and Bill Cosby, among others. Reading a book for *Reading Rainbow* is looked upon as an honor and joy for these celebrities. In fact, on several occasions, actors have refused payment!

What is the creative process involved in producing each episode?

Once the feature book is selected, the *Reading Rainbow* staff is ready to go. First, they extrapolate thematic ideas from the book. Then the producer, associate producer, director, writer, production assistants, and researchers work as a team to brainstorm extensions of the episode. They begin by asking questions like "What kinds of interviews and program segments would make this theme come alive on television?" "What would five-to-eight-year-olds want to know about the subject?" and "How could we best treat the topic so that kids will be so excited that they clamor for the featured books?"

Sometimes an episode points in one direction but ends up taking a completely different path. For example, the book *Nosey Mrs. Rat* is a story about someone who spies on her neighbors. The original idea was to focus the show on spying, with segments on the FBI and submarines. However, upon further discussion it was apparent that these ideas would not be appropriate for our audience because spying isn't nice. Therefore, the staff decided to take a more lighthearted approach and produce a show about curiosity, with a focus on watching and observing wildlife.

After a wealth of ideas have been generated, research begins. Every possibility is discussed and considered. As the field narrows, a plan for the show starts to come together. The writer then creates an outline which will be revised and developed, as the entire team molds the show concept into a script.

As the script is developed and several drafts are written, the production team also researches appropriate locations in which to shoot the show. The location must be consistent with the theme of the book and show. For example, a show about dinosaurs was shot at Dinosaur National Park in Jensen, Utah, and a program about the seashore was shot on location on the island of Upper Captiva in Florida.

Sometimes budgetary and time constraints mean that the best locations have to be replaced with something not quite so glamorous. For example, in the "Salamander Room" program, the rain forest location was shot at the Bronx Zoo/Wildlife Conservation Park's JungleWorld, a simulated rain forest. Originally, we had planned to shoot the segment in Costa Rica, but the costs and time involved to travel that far were prohibitive.

Once a final script is approved, the *Reading Rainbow* crew travels to the location to shoot LeVar's "wraps"—portions of the show called "wraparounds" in which LeVar introduces each new segment.

After the wraps are completed, all of the other show segments are shot. Each episode includes a television adaptation of the feature book, field segments, and a book review segment. The adaptation of the feature book is like a short film of the book, and includes the illustrations adapted to the screen, a celebrity narrator, sound effects, animation, and original music.

The field segments build on the ideas from the feature book and turn them into real-life adventures. *Reading Rainbow* field segments have transported viewers to many exciting locations, from inside the earth in the California Caverns (outside of San Francisco) to a Native American powwow at the Crow Fair in Crow Agency, Montana, to Chinatown in New York City. Also, through these field segments, viewers have met a variety of performers, scientists, naturalists, and other experts they wouldn't ordinarily have the chance to meet in their daily lives. Segments have included a twelve-year-old boy who started his own library, an interview with Whoopi Goldberg, musical performances by Ben Vereen, Pete Seeger, Sweet Honey in the Rock, and Run DMC, and interviews with three families created through adoption.

It's not always as glamorous as it may seem to work in television; take it from the *Reading Rainbow* crew! During most of the shoot for the episode "Seashore Surprises," for example, the crew was perched in mangrove trees while LeVar stood in the middle of a muddy swamp with bugs swarming around him.

At the shoot on Mount Kilauea in Hawaii, the crew taped while the volcano erupted! Toward the end of the shoot, the crew was told that they had to leave the volcano as soon as possible because the wind was changing and the helicopter couldn't fly if the wind became too strong. LeVar and most of the crew members made it out on time, but the wind shifted and the helicopter was grounded before the pilot could go back for the video technician and the sound technician. They ended up spending the night on the top of the volcano with a handful of scientists who were studying it.

On location at the San Diego Zoo, the crew planned to shoot the feature book's introductory wrap with a group of goats surrounding LeVar and trying to nibble on the book. The zoo staff told the crew and LeVar that goats didn't really eat paper (or everything that they saw). This was merely a myth. So in order to get the goats to stand near LeVar, the producer hid corn in all of LeVar's pockets. Not only did the goats hungrily attack LeVar, but they also munched the paperback copy of the feature book *Gregory the*

Terrible Eater that was in his back pocket.

Not only is work in television less than glamorous, but it is also exhausting. While shooting the episode entitled "Come a Tide," the script called for LeVar to lie in a hammock and look at clouds in the sky. Between takes, LeVar rested with his eyes shut. But when the director called action, LeVar's eyes stayed closed. At first everyone thought that he was just kidding, but LeVar had really fallen asleep.

The final element produced for each show is the book review segment. Nonprofessional children are auditioned and met with by the producers of *Reading Rainbow*. Children are then matched to one of the review books based on their personalities and interests and brought into the studio for an actual taping. With the help of an adult floor director, the children talk about the review book and write their own book reviews. There are usually two children assigned to every book, and the best review is then chosen to appear in the actual episode.

Once all of the segments are shot, the show is edited. And once the pictures are cut together, all of the "sweetening" occurs. Music, additional sound, special effects, animation, and other finishing touches are added to the show. Now the episode is ready for air on PBS.

How the 101 Best Titles Were Selected

By Cynthia Mayer Benfield

In the spring of 1993, Dr. Twila Liggett, executive producer of *Reading Rainbow*, asked me if I would like to compile a list of 100 of the "best" *Reading Rainbow* books for a guide for parents. I had been with *Reading Rainbow* for nine years and held the position of manager of literary properties. This job entailed seeking outstanding children's picture books, testing them among children ages five to nine, and, for those selected, acquiring literary rights to put these books on the air and in the *Reading Rainbow* booklist. As a teacher, I had continued contact with beginning readers, and I soon came to know what they consider a great book and what they absolutely will not sit through. However, narrowing the list of over 400 *Reading Rainbow* titles was challenging to say the least. When the list was finally boiled down to 101—58 feature books, 40 review books, and 3 highlight books—and I couldn't decide which one to delete, Dr. Liggett suggested we simply change the number to 101. Everyone agreed.

After consulting with several professionals in children's literature and education, many requirements clearly needed to be addressed. Most important, this list had to be comprised of quality books that children would indeed enjoy reading, rather than titles with attractive covers or moral endings which parents might *think* children would enjoy. Also, each book on the list had to be in print and available in bookstores and libraries.

This compilation had to be inclusive if it was to serve as a worthy introduction to literature for the young reader. Books could be silly, just for fun, serious, adventure, fantasy, or nonfiction. Many different literary styles have been included: storybook, poetry, reference book, chapter book, and also books whose text is bilingual on the page. Characters are multi-aged and multicultural, female, male, and oftentimes animal. There are new titles, not-so-new titles, and a few of the wonderful classics that will hopefully be familiar to the parents and caregivers of beginning readers. The goal is to interest every reader on many levels by offering a variety of reading subjects and styles. Each book is a noted artistic achievement and will delight the eye of the reader immediately and forever.

A great children's book is a pleasure to pick up, savor, and read. There are now, more than ever, numerous outstanding books available for children. Following is a list of the cream of the crop. One hundred and one books to curl up with and read, read, read! Of course, other titles belong on this list, but space allowed for only so many. Enjoy these and other titles by the same authors and illustrators, seek out new ones, and over time, let your own list grow.

Adventure

Alistair in Outer Space

By Marilyn Sadler,
illustrated by Roger Bollen
Prentice-Hall Books for Young Readers

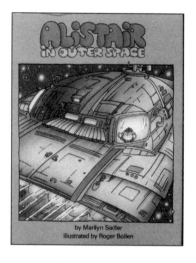

This just-for-fun, very silly story is about a fastidious boy whose iron-clad schedule is rocked when two alien Goots whisk him away in a spaceship. Full-color illustrations are droll and cartoonlike. Their large size and brightness will appeal to the youngest reader. Text is sparse, which only makes the story more succinct and funny.

"Alistair Grittle was a sensible boy. Every day he made a list of the things he had to do. Then he made a list of the things he did not have to do." One day, while returning his library books (on time, of course), something unusual happens: Two creatures, who call themselves Goots, take a liking to Alistair and decide to take him back to Gootula. "Alistair thanked the Goots very much." But he tells them, "My library books are due back today. The librarian will be expecting me." A series of wrong turns in space has Alistair worried that he'll have to pay a late fee on the books, so the Goots finally agree to return him to Earth.

Because Goots are not known to be very good with directions, Alistair takes over flying the ship. He spots Earth and is glad that he took that shortcut. With his face behind a pile of books, Alistair steps off the spaceship, relieved to be home, unaware that he is surrounded by penguins! This wonderfully ridiculous adventure will have children laughing from start to finish.

Program Description for
Alistair in Outer Space
(Show #706)*

LeVar goes on a treasure hunt in the Library of Congress in "Alistair in Outer Space." He looks at old maps and globes, and *A Trip to the Moon*, one of the first science fiction films, made almost a hundred years ago. Watch as old books are repaired: Their pages are washed in water to loosen the dirt and the sections are sewn back together by hand. The finishing touches are put on as books are bound in leather and the title is imprinted with gold leaf.

Step in to the animated world of "Conan the Librarian"— where a boy proves himself worthy of The Gift of the Sacred Card of the Library. Conan urges the boy to use this new tool to unlock the kingdom of books and learn their power.

---

*To find out when a *Reading Rainbow* program will be broadcast, please call your local PBS station and ask for it by show number and title. To order copies of *Reading Rainbow* videos, write: Reading Rainbow/GPN, PO Box 80669, Lincoln, NE 68501, or call 800-228-4630.

Mystery on the Docks
Written and illustrated by Thacher Hurd
HarperCollins

In this exciting, tongue-in-cheek mystery, Ralph, an opera-loving short-order cook at a diner, witnesses two shady-looking rats kidnapping his favorite singer. When he is captured and thrown into the hold of a ship with Eduardo, the singer, they must find a way out before it's too late! Their kidnapping and rescue on the high seas are told with great humor and matched by colorful yet darkly mysterious illustrations. The slinky

rats prove to be outwitted, and children will cheer for Ralph, a rodent who won't give up until he's rid of those no-good, dirty rats.

Singing, as he loves to do, Ralph the rat is just ending his night shift at the diner on Pier 46 when two rats slink into the place, rudely demand food, and then leave without paying. When Ralph chases them, they capture him and put him in the hold of *Dark Ship* with another kidnapped victim, Eduardo Bombasto, world-renowned opera-singing rat! Oh, no! When the two run up the mast, sending flares into the night sky for help, they find it is too foggy. What next? "I can sing!" exclaims Eduardo. "HALLLPP!" The police hear his call and come running. Big Al and his good-for-nothing rats are taken to the slammer, and Ralph enjoys a front-row seat at Eduardo's concert that night.

Program Description for
"Mystery on the Docks"
(Show #204)

Sporting a trench coat and a fedora, LeVar is in Charleston Harbor on the trail of Big Momma Blue in "Mystery on the Docks." He finds her on the wharf—she's a huge crane used to load and unload freighters. The name Big Momma Blue was given to her by the city's schoolchildren. Some of the freighters are as high as a sixteen-story building and as long as three football fields!

Viewers get an up-close tour of another key player in harbor life, the tugboat. These little boats, sometimes one-ninth the size of the freighters, help maneuver the bigger ships in and out of port. The song "I Am a Tugboat Captain" accompanies two tugboats as they guide a ship into the harbor.

Watch the Stars Come Out

By Riki Levinson, illustrated by Diane Goode
E. P. Dutton, a division of Penguin Books USA Inc.

This is a special story about a little red-haired girl and her brother braving it on their own on a voyage across the ocean to join their family in America in the 1800s. The warm, humorous text and luminous illustrations underscore the value of sharing family history over and over again for younger generations to remember and pass on to their own children.

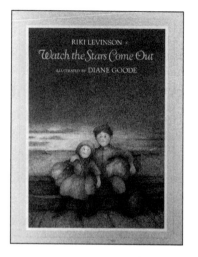

Grandma tells the story about her mama as a little girl, arriving at the pier: She and her brother are ready to board the ship and begin their journey. "Aunt gave us a barrel full of dried fruit. She asked an old lady to watch over us. And she did. She also ate our dried fruit." The trip turns out to be quite an adventure. Some of the things that happen are sad. "Some people didn't like it—they got sick. The old lady got very, very sick. She died. Brother told me not to worry. He would take care of me—he was ten." When bad weather forces the passengers to stay below decks, the overcrowded conditions make the girl yearn to see the vast starry sky.

Twenty-three days later, they see two islands! One of them has a statue of a woman standing on it. Everyone cheers. They pass through Immigration and then finally arrive on the mainland. There are Mama and Papa and Sister! That night, in their new "palace," the little girl lies in her warm, spacious bed, appreciating the beautiful view from her window. She counts the stars as they come out: one, two, three.

Program Description for
"Watch the Stars Come Out"
(Show #309)

In "Watch the Stars Come Out," LeVar explores the stories, icons, and cultures of American immigrants. First-person narratives enrich archival footage of people arriving at Ellis Island. While the Statue of Liberty gets a facelift for her one-hundredth birthday, LeVar sees eye-to-eye with Miss Liberty when he joins the renovation crew up on the scaffolding.

Immigrants share their first impressions of the United States, its citizens and food. At an ethnic festival, viewers have a front-row seat for performances by Irish step dancers, a Puerto Rican folklorico musical group, and Caribbean stilt-dancing from the Virgin Islands. Neil Diamond's popular song "America" is brought to life with images from Ellis Island and the ethnic festival.

Animals

Arthur's Eyes
Written and illustrated by Marc Brown
Atlantic Monthly Press/Little, Brown and Co.

Needing glasses in the second grade can be traumatic. In this irresistibly funny yet sympathetic story, Arthur the aardvark has to decide which is worse: getting headaches, bumping into walls, and missing baskets in gym; or being teased and called Four-Eyes by his classmates. When his empathetic, bespectacled teacher gives him a few words of encouragement, Arthur gains the courage to face the world with 20/20 vision.

When his optometrist prescribes glasses, Arthur picks out some fashionable frames and is delighted to be able to see clearly. However, at the bus stop the next morning, the other children call him names. Poor Arthur. So embarrassed is he that he decides to lose his glasses. Without them a trip to the bathroom that day results in hilarious havoc when Arthur, who counted the doors as he went along to be sure of entering the right room, finds Francine inside. "What was Francine doing in the boys' room? 'Get out of here!' screamed Francine. 'This is the girls' room!'" Arthur is mortified. That afternoon, he speaks with his teacher, who informs Arthur that he too wears glasses, for reading. "He took them out. They looked just like Arthur's. . . . Suddenly Arthur felt better."

With glasses on, Arthur is able to shoot ten baskets in gym (Francine makes four). He gets every math problem on the blackboard right (Francine misses two), and when Francine asks Arthur to be on her team after school, Arthur says, "I'll consider it." Soon other children want to wear glasses like Arthur. This helps him see, clearly, that he's made the right decision.

Program Description for
"Arthur's Eyes"
(Show #113)

"Arthur's Eyes" is all about ways of seeing. Close-up views of colorful illustrations challenge viewers' powers of observation and pose riddles for the eyes. Maya Angelou narrates a photo-essay inspired by Arnold Adoff's "All the Colors of the Race"—poems about how "the real color is behind the color . . . under that skin and under that face is the real race."

Young filmmakers listen to classical music and animate their visions of the music—a ballerina in blue, dancing dominoes, and colorful shapes that change like a kaleidoscope. LeVar explains how blind people read with their hands, and meets a group of mimes who show how much you can say without speaking a word.

Dabble Duck

By Anne Leo Ellis
Illustrated by Sue Truesdell
HarperCollins

When a boy and his best duck friend are forced to be parted each day, they find that including a third friend can take away the loneliness and actually make the friendship grow stronger. This is a heartwarming story, cheerily illustrated in Sue Truesdell's eminent style, that reminds us that our friendship with people *or* animals is the most important thing we can have.

Dabble has lived with Jason since she was tiny. Now a big white duck, Dabble misses Jason when he goes to school every day, and she makes a mess of the apartment to prove it! In the park one afternoon, Jason watches his friends play with Dabble. "A little black dog was watching too. His fur was tangled and dirty. His right ear was torn. But he sat with a big dog smile and wagged his tail." The dog follows Dabble when it's time to go home, and Jason notices that the dog is limping. "Oh, dog, your leg must hurt a lot, and you look hungry! I think you need a friend." And so it comes to be that the little dog, whom Dabble has affectionately named Quack, is welcomed into the family, cared for, and becomes good company for Dabble, offering the perfect solution for keeping friends together.

Please refer to the program description for "The Runaway Duck." *Dabble Duck* **is a Review Book in this episode.**

Make Way for Ducklings

Written and illustrated by Robert McCloskey
Viking Kestrel, a division of Penguin Books USA Inc.

In 1941, Robert McCloskey wrote a delightful story about a duck family that finds a place to call home in the city of Boston, Massachusetts. This unique tale, illustrated in black and white, is a wonderful reminder of days gone by and is absolutely appropriate for young readers of today. Every child should have the pleasure of knowing this true classic.

Mr. and Mrs. Mallard are looking for a place to raise their family. After a tour of Boston proper, they settle on a nice, quiet island in the Charles River. Michael, a policeman, feeds them peanuts every day. When eight ducklings—Jack, Kack, Lack, Mack, Nack, Ouack, Pack, and Quack—finally hatch, it's time for the family to move again.

Officer Michael paves the way to the Public Garden as Mrs. Mallard, with all her ducks in a row, makes the trek. "He planted himself in the center of the road, raised one hand to stop the traffic, and then beckoned with the other, the way policemen do, for Mrs. Mallard to cross over." Arriving safely in the Boston Public Garden, Mrs. Mallard and her ducklings find Mr. Mallard "waiting for them, just as he had promised." And that is where they live and play for all of their days.

Program Description for
"Stay Away From the Junkyard"
(Show #602)

(*Make Way for Ducklings* is a Review Book in this episode.)

In "Stay Away From the Junkyard," LeVar tries to clean out his garage, but keeps finding things he can't bear to get rid of and ends up taking a trip down memory lane. Viewers see LeVar's high school yearbook, baby pictures, and some of his all-time favorite books. In the end, LeVar finds the only thing he doesn't need is his "Yard Sale" sign! Kids talk about special belongings they can't let go. Book reviews highlight classic stories to remember forever.

Artist Michael Ives shows how he's made recycling an art. A world-class "scrounger," Michael saves all kinds of objects and finds ways to use them in a sculpture. Making a "storybox," Michael starts with an old drawer. Inside it, using only paint and items from his junkyard, he creates a fantastic Old West rodeo scene, complete with a bucking bronco.

Raccoons and Ripe Corn

Written and illustrated by Jim Arnosky
Lothrop, Lee & Shepard Books

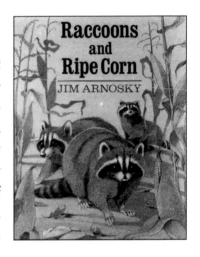

Noted author-artist and naturalist Jim Arnosky offers a poetic glimpse of wildlife that is rarely seen: raccoons munching on tender, ripe corn right off the stalk, in this simply beautiful nature book for the very young reader. This is one in a series of four books, which highlight deer, muskrat, and fox in their natural environments. These dramatic scenes are riveting. Lifelike illustrations adorn each page. Little text is used. For the child interested in seeing wild creatures in real life, this is an excellent reference book.

In autumn, when the leaves turn color and the corn is plump and ripe, a mother raccoon and her two kits sneak into the cornfield. "They climb the tall stalks and pull the ears down to the ground, they peel away the green husk that covers the yellow kernels. All night long the raccoons feast on corn. . . . At sunrise, the raccoons hurry back into the woods." This is a visual field trip for every young naturalist.

Program Description for
"Raccoons and Ripe Corn"
"Deer at the Brook"
"Come Out, Muskrats"
(Show #802)

LeVar goes to Ramtails Farm to meet Jim Arnosky in "Raccoons and Ripe Corn." In addition to the title book, two of Arnosky's other stories are adapted for television: *Deer at the Brook* and *Come Out, Muskrats.* Jim shows LeVar how to be a wildlife detective. Armed with binoculars and waders, the two set off to look for clues that an animal has been nearby.

By the brook, Jim points out raccoon paw prints in the mud. He knows the animal didn't stop for a drink, because the tracks show a walking pattern and no side trip to the water. Jim says the best way to sneak up on wildlife is to get low and "pretend you're a stump." At an aspen tree, Jim spots claw marks that mean a porcupine climbed this tree. LeVar watches as he sketches what that scene might have looked like.

The Story of Ferdinand

By Munro Leaf
Illustrated by Robert Lawson
Viking Penguin, a division of Penguin Books USA Inc.

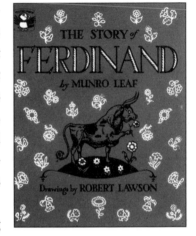

We are all individuals. The importance of being unique and different is told wisely here in a refreshing, sweet story. Written in 1936, this is a classic tale, timeless in its message and its appeal. For all his size and strength, Ferdinand the bull is gentle and peace-loving. Black-and-white illustrations express all of Ferdinand's emotions as beautifully as the text.

Instead of running and jumping and butting heads with the other bulls, Ferdinand is content to sit quietly in the pasture under a cork tree and smell the flowers. When he is chosen to be El Toro Feroz, the fiercest bull of all, to fight at the bullfight in Madrid, he decides to do what he does best—he sits in the center of the ring and smells all the flowers from the hair of the lovely ladies watching, *much* to the displeasure of the matador. Ferdinand knows what makes him happy and, in his gentle way, achieves this goal; he is not at all afraid to be different. Take the time to stop, smell the flowers, and enjoy this refreshing tale.

Please refer to program description for "Stay Away From the Junkyard." *The Story of Ferdinand* **is a Review Book in this episode.**

Concepts

Growing Vegetable Soup
Written and illustrated by Lois Ehlert
Harcourt Brace

Father and child do everything possible with a vegetable garden, from planting seeds to making soup, in this extremely attractive story. The text is oversized and spare, amplified by huge neon-colored collage illustrations. The art fills each page from the ground's point of view; human hands are present, but even they are working in the dirt. All of the tools and vegetables are labeled.

"Dad said we are going to grow vegetable soup." Tools in hand, the two plant the seeds, water and weed, and watch their garden grow. Once the vegetables are big and ripe, they are ready for picking (or digging up). "Then we wash them and cut them into vegetable soup!" Never before have father and child tasted anything so delicious. And to think they can grow it again next year! The reader doesn't have to wait quite as long, for this story can be enjoyed during any season.

Program Description for
"June 29, 1999"
(Show #1005)

(*Growing Vegetable Soup* is a Review Book in this episode.)

The book adaptation in "June 29, 1999" is all about a girl who thinks her science experiment has gone awry when giant vegetables float down to earth, blanketing the planet in produce. On a spooky night in a creepy old library, LeVar has a helping hand as he explores phenomena that have perplexed people for years. Kids guess what is "fact or fiction."

Dramatic reenactments take viewers to the moments when a woman sees a UFO and a boy discovers a dinosaur bone. Farmer Howard Dill shares the secrets of his success growing award-winning—enormous!—pumpkins. A look at unidentified flying objects and the people who've seen them will leave viewers searching the night skies.

How to Dig a Hole to the Other Side of the World

by Faith McNulty
Illustrated by Marc Simont
HarperCollins

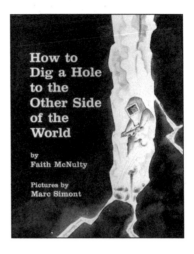

If you have ever wanted to dig a hole to China, this book will give you the real story. Join an ambitious child as he travels through each layer of the earth to get to the opposite side. Imaginative text and illustrations that vary from close-up to moon's-eye-view capture the enormous task of traveling eight thousand miles. Every child deserves to go on this wild journey. This unusual book makes it possible.

"Find a soft place. Take a shovel and start to dig a hole." Keep digging through layer upon layer, ever mindful of what you might find. "The bones of many animals—dinosaurs, giant tigers, turtles, and other creatures of long ago—are buried everywhere. If you find some, dust them off carefully and save them." You may hit water. You may even hit oil. Keep drilling; through basalt, through magma. "To go through red-hot magma you will need a jet-propelled submarine. It must have a super cooling system, a fireproof skin and a drill at the tip of its nose." At this point, you're only halfway there.

Approximately two thousand miles later, you'll hit the center of the earth, "a place where east meets west, north meets south and up meets down. At the center of the earth there is nothing under you. Every direction is up. . . . Do not stay long. Go straight ahead and begin the long trip up." This is a delightful and highly imaginative story which will answer even the most precocious and inquisitive child's questions.

Please refer to the program description for "The Magic School Bus Inside the Earth." *How to Dig a Hole to the Other Side of the World* **is a Review Book in this episode.**

If You Give a Mouse a Cookie

By Laura Joffe Numeroff
Illustrated by Felicia Bond
HarperCollins

This delightful, silly story introduces the young reader to the concept of things coming full circle. Like a chain of tumbling dominoes, one thing leads to another and finally brings us back to where we started again. The instigator of all this is a perfectly adorable and charming little mouse who endears himself to his host, a young boy, who is eager to please his guest—no matter *what* the consequences.

"If you give a mouse a cookie, he's going to ask for a glass of milk. When you give him the milk, he'll probably ask you for a straw. When he's finished, he'll ask for a napkin. Then he'll want to look in a mirror to make sure he doesn't have a milk mustache. When he looks in the mirror, he might ask for a pair of scissors. . . ." Through the house they go, creating and accomplishing task after task until, exhausted, the mouse finds that he is thirsty. "So . . . he'll ask for a glass of milk. And chances are if he asks for a glass of milk, he's going to want a cookie to go with it."

Program Description for
"If You Give a Mouse a Cookie"
(Show #1002)

Exploring how one thing leads to another, LeVar goes bowling in "If You Give a Mouse a Cookie." Bowling is a cycle too—throw the ball, the ball hits the pins, the pins fall down, get pushed onto a wheel that takes them up to the pinsetter, they fall into place and are lowered to the floor again so you can throw another ball and start all over.

In a behind-the-scenes look at how bowling balls are made, viewers get a glimpse at another chain reaction in progress—an assembly line. The final piece is a visit with Bob Speca, "Domino Wizard." Bob demonstrates his steady-handed technique for stacking dominoes, including patterns called "Centipede" and "Six Days Till Sunday."

Opt: An Illusionary Tale

Written and illustrated by Arline and Joseph Baum
Viking Penguin, a division of Penguin Books USA Inc.

How we look at things can affect the way we see, and sometimes our eyes play tricks on us. Here is an engaging collection of optical illusions and puzzles for the mind, cleverly told in storybook format. Follow the Jester of the court as he leads us from page to page, introducing a new puzzle, optical illusion, or way of seeing that the reader has never experienced before. This is the perfect book to share with a family member or a friend. And don't worry, all the illusions are explained at the end.

Opt is the name of a kingdom where something magical is happening all the time. In the blink of an eye, images will appear and disappear. Illusions unfold one after the other as the reader follows the Jester on an unusual path to meet the king and queen for a special celebration. Objects shift color and size for no reason at all, only for the reader to find that there is, indeed, reason. Instructions for making your own optical illusions are provided as well.

Program Description for
"Opt: An Illusionary Tale"
(Show #801)

Optical illusions are everywhere in "Opt." LeVar is climbing a mountain in a raging snowstorm—or is he? LeVar explains the technology of TV's favorite illusion.

Trompe l'oeil (that's "trick the eye" in French) is the art of illusion practiced by Christian Thee. He shows viewers simple ways to fool the eye with line drawings, and also creates a beautiful carnival that looks so real you can almost hear it. Some of the most intricate illusions of all are found in nature. A close-up look at animal camouflage reveals stunning adaptations that help creatures large and small play "hide and seek."

Emotions

Alexander and the Terrible, Horrible, No Good, Very Bad Day

By Judith Viorst
Illustrated by Ray Cruz
Atheneum

Did you ever have one of those days where things just go from bad to worse? The boy in this story watches his day deteriorate before his very eyes. Black-and-white pen-and-ink drawings express each mishap in a funny, sensitive way that offers the reader the comfort of knowing that some days are like that—for all of us.

Poor Alexander, he knows that this is going to be a terrible, horrible, no good, very bad day. Gum that was in his mouth last night is in his hair when he wakes up. At breakfast, his brothers each find prizes in their cereal boxes. Alexander only finds cereal. And that's just the beginning. "I think I'll move to Australia," he says. School is no better. His teacher informs him during counting time that he left out the number sixteen. "Who needs sixteen?" he thinks to himself, miserably. It's definitely time to go to Australia.

Lima beans for dinner. Yuck! Kissing on TV. Double yuck! When's the next flight to Australia? Mercifully, Alexander's day ends, and at bedtime, his understanding mother informs him that some days are like that . . . even in Australia. Share this reassuring story with the child who's had an all-around rotten, no good, very bad day.

Please refer to the program description for "The Day Jimmy's Boa Ate the Wash." *Alexander and the Terrible, Horrible, No Good, Very Bad Day* **is a Review Book in this episode.**

Dakota Dugout

By Ann Turner
Illustrated by Ronald Himler
Macmillan Publishing Co.

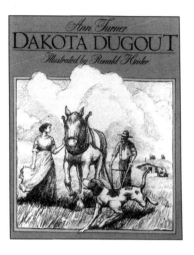

In this remarkable story, a grand-mother eloquently describes for her granddaughter what it was like to cope with pioneer life on the Dakota prairie one hundred years ago. Poetic text is complemented by sensitive line drawings that capture the essence of a lonely, barren existence that a young couple must endure in order to survive. The difficulties they face and their achievements offer a rare and unforgettable experience to every reader.

When the letter arrives saying "Come!" the young bride packs up quickly and travels to the Dakotas to join her new husband. Matt has built a sod house for them and it makes her cry when she sees it. Lonely, with only animals to keep them company, the couple must work endlessly to prepare for the coming winter. A blizzard wipes out half their cattle. The following summer, the crops are baked dry in a drought. Disheartened but determined, Matt and his bride keep at it until, finally, one summer the crops take hold and the couple is able to "build a clapboard house with windows like suns." Prosperous now, the woman never forgets that period of her life, when love for each other was the only thing they could count on. Mindful of this, she tells her granddaughter, "Sometimes the things we start with are best."

Please refer to the program description for "Meanwhile Back at the Ranch." *Dakota Dugout* is a Review Book in this episode.

Feelings

By Aliki
Greenwillow Books

It's not always easy to express our feelings. Realizing this, Aliki has created a handbook of emotions for kids; complete and illustrated, it will provide lots of comfort and a few giggles, no matter what the reader's mood. Each page is a chapter in itself, ranging in topic from anger, jealousy, and fear to pride, joy, and love. Here, children interact with other children, in pictures, dialogues, poems, and stories to portray the various emotions we all feel.

One page shows a young girl standing in front of a classroom, thinking to herself, "I'd like to hide. They're all staring at me. Is she laughing at me? I wish I could fall through the crack in the floor." Meanwhile, bubble text from her classmates indicates *their* feelings, "She looks shy," "You'd feel shy, too, if you were standing up there," "She looks nice." And finally in the concluding picture, "Hello, my name is Patricia." A friend at last!

Another delightful two-page spread shows a little boy, lying in the grass, alone, with a picnic and a stream nearby. He's holding his teddy bear. This example is entitled "feeling quiet." There are a host of other scenarios presented. Positive or negative, this book will help children to identify their feelings and express themselves accordingly.

Program Description for
"Feelings"
(Show #308)

The book adaptation in "Feelings" is fully animated, and vignettes appear throughout the show as "bumpers" between segments. A composer directs a chorus of children sounding out emotions with their voices, but not in words.

Animals have feelings too, and Koko, a nine-year-old mountain gorilla, talks about it in American Sign Language (ASL). Keeper and friend Penny Patterson speaks with Koko in ASL, and interprets what she signs. Koko is sad because her kitten died, but when Penny finds her a new playmate, Koko is thrilled. The music video "With a Friend" captures moments when people are sharing smiles and good times.

A Gift for Tía Rosa

By Karen T. Taha
Illustrated by Dee deRosa
Gemstone Books, a division of Dillon Press,
Inc.

This is an emotional book about a young Latino girl who must deal with the loss of her elderly next-door neighbor. Little Carmela and Tía Rosa, dear friends, spend a great deal of time laughing, talking, and knitting together. In a very short period of time, Tía Rosa becomes ill and then dies. Carmela and the others left behind must find a way to get through this period. Soon thereafter, Tía Rosa's first granddaughter is born, providing just the inspiration they all need.

"Around, over, through, and pull," repeats Carmela as she knits a rainbow-colored scarf for her father's Christmas present. Her neighbor Tía Rosa taught her how to knit, and now Carmela can't wait for Tía Rosa to get home from the hospital to help her add the fringe. Her parents discourage a visit so soon, but a call from Tía Rosa that evening brings Carmela running next door. When she gets there, Carmela sees that, for the first time since they met eight years ago, Tía Rosa is in bed! Nevertheless, "hugging Tía Rosa always made Carmela feel safe and warm. Tía Rosa was like a soft pillow that smelled of soap and bath powder and sometimes of sweet tamales. Now there was another smell, a dentist office smell, Carmela decided."

Every day after school, and on weekends, Carmela visits Tía Rosa. Together they knit; the scarf for Carmela's father and a baby blanket for Tía Rosa's not-yet-born grandchild. One evening, Tía Rosa gives Carmela a gift, a tiny silver rose on a fine chain. "The rose is so you'll remember your old Tía Rosa," says the elder. "How could I forget you, Tía Rosa?" asks Carmela. "You're right here!" But soon, Tía Rosa isn't home anymore. A call from Tío Juan, Rosa's husband, informs them that they have lost Tía Rosa.

A time of grief follows. Carmela wishes she had given a gift to her friend. "Carmela, Tía Rosa didn't want her kindness returned. She wanted it passed on," says her mother. "That way a part of Tía Rosa will never die." This gives Carmela an idea. When Rosa's grandchild is born, Carmela takes the unfinished blanket and begins, "around, over, through, and pull . . . at last she has a gift for Tía Rosa."

Program Description for
"Best Friends"
(Show #413)

(*A Gift for Tía Rosa* is a Review Book in this episode.)

The book adaptation in "Best Friends" tells the tale of a little girl, her very best friend, a kind old neighbor, and his dog. LeVar embarks on a "dog show" all about man's relationship with his "best friend." Viewers meet Beth, a little girl who's a "puppy walk-er" for Leader Dogs for the Blind. She takes care of a puppy named Abbey for a year until the dog is old enough to start working with a blind person. When the time comes to give up Abbey, Beth is very sad. But when she sees Elaine, the woman Abbey is going to help, Beth feels much better.

At a dog show, canine contestants strut their stuff. But the real show is behind the scenes, as owners groom their pets and get them ready for the limelight. The song "A Perfect Match" highlights especially interesting dogs and their people. And there's one unusual book reviewer who's doggone good. . . .

Molly's Pilgrim

By Barbara Cohen
Illustrated by Michael J. Deraney
Lothrop, Lee & Shepard Books

When a young immigrant girl com-
pletes her school project and is taunt-
ed by her classmates for being different, she learns that it takes a
tremendous amount of strength to
rise above such unjust prejudice.
Black-and-white illustrations set the
tone of this story, which is based on
truth.

Molly is a young Jewish immi-
grant from Russia. At school, everyone in the class is asked to make
a Pilgrim doll for the class's Thanksgiving display. With Mama's
help, the project is complete. But wait, the doll looks like Mama!
"Mama's smile turned into a laugh. 'Of course. I did that on pur-
pose.' 'You did, Mama? Why?' 'What's a Pilgrim, Shaynkeit?'
Mama asked. 'A Pilgrim is someone who came here from the other
side to find freedom. That's me, Molly. I'm a Pilgrim!' "

Still apprehensive, Molly brings the doll to school and finds
she is tormented by her classmates because her doll looks so different. Miss Stickley, their teacher, calls them to order and explains
that Molly's doll *is* a Pilgrim, a modern Pilgrim. And that the early
Pilgrims got the idea for Thanksgiving from the story in the bible
about the Jewish highest holiday of Tabernacles—Succoth.

Finally, Miss Stickley asks if she may put Molly's Pilgrim on
her desk, "where everyone can see it all the time. It will remind us

all that Pilgrims are still coming to America." It is then that Molly realizes that she has done the right thing and that it takes all kinds of Pilgrims to make a Thanksgiving.

Please refer to the program description for "Watch the Stars Come Out." *Molly's Pilgrim* **is a Review Book in this episode.**

A Three Hat Day

By Laura Geringer
Illustrated by Arnold Lobel
HarperCollins

This is a modern fairy tale in which an eccentric and lonely man, with a passion for hats, finds true love when he least expects it. Ever so gently told, this darling story has a rhythmic pace that readers will find soothing. The illustrations are funny and charming. For the reader interested in hats *or* love, this is a story not to be missed.

R. R. Pottle the Third loved hats. He was the last of a long line of Pottles. His father had collected canes; his mother, umbrellas. Together, they took long walks in the rain. Now, only R.R. lived in the Pottle mansion, and he was lonely. "He dreamed of meeting his future wife in the rain. And he dreamed she would be wearing the perfect hat."

One morning R.R. felt so sad, he put on not one, not two, but three hats at once and went into town, hoping to cheer himself up. Finding himself in a hat store, he did feel a little better. Just when he was leaving, a small woman came out from behind a curtain. "When she saw R.R., she smiled. It was the sweetest smile he had ever seen. And above the smile was a hat. A *perfect* hat! On one side, a sequin seal balanced a shiny ball on the tip of its nose. On the other, tiny gold bells jangled. And a plume as soft and grey as fog graced the peak." Quietly, R.R. asked the woman if she would like to take a walk—in the rain. Ever after they lived in the Pottle mansion, where R. R. Pottle the Fourth was born. She loved shoes!

Program Description for
"A Three Hat Day"
(Show #411)

LeVar finds an unusual hat shop in "A Three Hat Day." In this store, it's not what you wear, but where it takes you. By putting on a "funny-looking baseball cap," LeVar ends up as a jockey on a horse named Wally Sombrero—and he wins the race. Next LeVar tries an engineer's hat. Instead of driving a locomotive, LeVar finds himself in Three Bridges, New Jersey, at one of the world's largest model railroads. This train set runs through six rooms and takes eighty-one people to operate.

His final hat trick sends LeVar to a practice session with the New York Islanders. He gets pointers on how to goaltend from Kelly Rhudy. And the perfect way to cap off this day? A knight's helmet that puts LeVar in full armor, ready to go jousting.

Environment

Come a Tide

By George Ella Lyon
Illustrated by Stephen Gammell
Orchard Books

When natural disaster strikes, one town bands together, putting forth a positive attitude and even a sense of humor to get through the ordeal. Repetitive, lyrical text is supported by humorous illustrations in an engaging book about flooding that depicts the severity of the disaster while giving each victim, animals included, a lighthearted we'll-get-through-this-together outlook. Not to be missed are the pigs floating by with contented smiles on their faces.

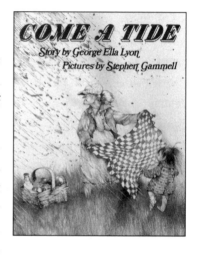

"It'll come a tide," says Grandma, who's lived long enough to know that after snow and four days of rain in March, a flood is bound to ensue. Ensue it does and kinfolk must gather together at Grandma's house up on the hill. "Rain came down like curtains as we drove up Grandma's hill. She fed us warmed-over biscuits and coffee stout as a post. Then she sent us to bed." When daylight comes, the rain is gone and Grandma suggests that everyone "make friends with a shovel" to unbury their treasures. A warm lunch from the rescue wagon shows everyone with smiles on their faces. Surviving a natural disaster is made easier for this town when a sense of humor, positive outlook, and caring friends all come together to meet a common goal.

Program Description for
"Come a Tide"
(Show #901)

"Come a Tide" takes a look at people who weathered one of the biggest natural disasters, Hurricane Hugo. The storm is followed every step of the way, with a focus on Charleston, South Carolina. As the town prepares to meet Hugo, and all the way through the massive clean-up left in his wake, the program emphasizes the strength of people who work together to help each other.

Breathtaking footage of incredible weather events reminds viewers why it's smart to stay inside when the forecast is foul. Awesome lightning strikes, towering tornadoes, and raging floods are just a few of the phenomena spotlighted.

The Great Kapok Tree: A Tale of the Amazon Rain Forest

Written and illustrated by Lynne Cherry
Gulliver Books/Harcourt Brace

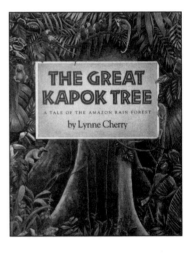

This is a story about conservation in the Amazon rain forest in Brazil, in which a community of animals living in one of its great kapok trees convinces a man with an ax to defer from chopping down their tree. Lynne Cherry wrote this book to give readers a glimpse of the incredible beauty of the rain forest and the creatures that inhabit it. Her watercolor illustrations are lush and memorable. The book is a disturbing reminder that the rain forest is being destroyed at an alarming rate and is a lesson to us all that the rain forest's destruction must stop.

In the dense, green Amazon rain forest, a man is told to chop down one of the great kapok trees. This tree grows tall enough to give sunlight to the dwellers of its highest branches and is so strongly rooted that darkness-preferring creatures may settle there. When the man tires from his chopping, he rests under the tree and in a dream he is approached by all of the tree's inhabitants, imploring him to stop.

A boa constrictor slithers down the tree trunk to the man and hisses, "Senhor, this tree is a tree of miracles. It is my home, where generations of my ancestors have lived. Do not chop it down." A toucan flies down from the canopy and squawks to the man, "You must not cut down this tree. We have flown over the rain forest and seen what happens once you begin to chop down the trees. Many people settle on the land. They set fires to clear the underbrush, and soon the forest disappears. Where there once was life and beauty only black and smoldering ruins remain."

Finally, a child from the Yanomama tribe murmurs in the man's ear: "Senhor, when you awake, please look at us with new eyes." The man wakes up, still seeing all the wondrous and rare creatures of his dream, drops his ax, and walks out of the rain forest. We all have much to gain from reading this hopeful story.

Please refer to the program description for "The Salamander Room." *The Great Kapok Tree: A Tale of the Amazon Rain Forest* **is a Review Book in this episode.**

The Salamander Room

By Anne Mazer
Illustrated by Steve Johnson
Alfred A. Knopf

See man adapt to nature in this remarkable, innocent story about a boy who finds a salamander and explains to his mother the many ways he could adapt his bedroom to accommodate the salamander's needs. Steve Johnson's illustrations are brilliant. The lush green bedroom scene unfolds, inviting mother to comply, and readers' imaginations to go wild.

When Brian finds a little orange salamander on the forest floor, he picks it up and invites it to live with him. When his mother asks where the salamander will sleep, the boy answers, "I will make him a salamander bed to sleep in. I will cover him with leaves that are fresh and green, and bring moss that looks like little stars to be a pillow for his head. I will bring crickets to sing him to sleep and bullfrogs to tell him good-night stories." On the boy goes, explaining where the salamander will play, what friends he'll bring the salamander to keep him from becoming lonely, and what food he'll provide. Brian's room magically and progressively transforms into the forest where he found the salamander, with one addition: a bed for Brian. See how beautiful life can be in this sweet book where nature plays the most important role.

Program Description for
"The Salamander Room"
(Show #909)

In "The Salamander Room," LeVar takes viewers on a guided tour of JungleWorld, a tropical rain forest in New York City. This spectacular habitat at the Bronx Wildlife Conservation Park was created with great care and attention to detail.

A naturalist explains why the plants and other elements of the exhibits are important to the animals who live there, including jaguars, tapirs, gibbons, and more. Viewers learn about how JungleWorld was made (including footage of its construction), and see how everything in the rain forest is interconnected, and why it's necessary to care for all parts of the ecosystem.

Fairy Tales, Folktales, Fables, and Legends

The Gift of the Sacred Dog

Written and illustrated by Paul Goble
Bradbury Press, an affiliate of Macmillan Publishing Co.

This boldly illustrated legend set in the Great Plains tells how the horse came to the Indians of North America. Paul Goble once again shares with the reader a fascinating account of Native American legend and culture. His well-known style of pen-and-ink and watercolor paintings bursts off the pages in full color, providing a spectacular and riveting story.

THE GIFT OF THE SACRED DOG
By PAUL GOBLE

When the people walk for many days and still find no buffalo to satisfy their hunger, a boy in the camp tells his parents, "I am sad to see everyone suffering. The dogs are hungry too. I am going up into the hills to ask the Great Spirit to help us. Do not worry about me; I shall return in the morning." Reaching the top of the highest hill, he makes his plea and then waits for a response. Suddenly the clouds part and a beautiful animal appears. "There was thunder in its nostrils and lightning in its legs; its eyes shone like stars and hair on its neck and tail trailed like clouds. The boy had never seen an animal so magnificent."

The next day dozens of "Sacred Dogs" follow him to the camp circle. The boy tells his people, "These are Sacred Dogs. They are a gift from the Great Spirit. They will help us to follow the buffalo and they will carry the hunters into the running herds. Now there will always be enough to eat. We must look after them well and they will be happy to live with us." And so the people live as relatives with the Sacred Dogs and all other living things, just as the Great Spirit had intended.

Program Description for
"The Gift of the Sacred Dog"
(Show #110)

LeVar visits the rolling plains of Montana in "The Gift of the Sacred Dog." Poetry is brought to life with footage of Native Americans on horseback. On a visit to Crow Fair, viewers meet Dan Old Elk and his family. Dan explains the traditions of this powwow, and his son helps set up a tepee and talks about the pride he feels in dancing.

A music video combines stunning landscapes and archival photos of Native Americans. Sung by Phoebe Snow, "Ancient Places, Sacred Names" reminds viewers how modern cities like Chicago and Miami got their names. Children share the names they'd give themselves—including Pink Fish and Reader.

The Legend of the Indian Paintbrush
Retold and illustrated by Tomie dePaola
G. P. Putnam's Sons

In his eminent style, Tomie dePaola retells the Native American legend about the journey of a young Indian boy who seeks to find that special gift he can give his people.

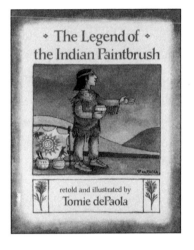

Little Gopher is not like the other boys. Unable to keep up with their running, riding, and wrestling, he's much more content decorating stones and wood with the red juice from berries found in the hills. When Little Gopher becomes a man, he continues with his talents, encouraged by a Dream-Vision, painting hides that the other men bring home from their hunts with colors from berries and flowers. But these colors are never as vivid as the colors of his Dream-Vision.

One evening, Little Gopher goes to the top of the hill as the colors of the sunset spread across the sky. "And there, on the ground all around him, were brushes filled with paint. Each one a color of the sunset. Little Gopher began to paint quickly and surely, using one brush, then another." When he finishes, Little Gopher leaves the brushes on the hillside, taking his beautiful painting down to the Circle of the People. The next day, the hill is ablaze with color, for the brushes have taken root in the earth and multiplied. And this has happened every spring since then.

Program Description for
"The Legend of the Indian Paintbrush"
(Show #708)

LeVar visits with the Pueblo people of New Mexico for a look at Native American arts in "The Legend of the Indian Paintbrush." Dominic Arquero, a buckskin artist from the Cochiti Pueblo, paints a glorious sunset and says his inspiration comes from his memory of all the sunsets he's ever seen. The Naranjo family—Dolly and her mother and daughter—come from the Santa Clara Pueblo, and share with viewers their special way of making pottery. Dolly talks about how pottery is their connection to the earth, and that they always respect the clay nature has given them.

The Taos Pueblo has been home to the Red Willow People for over one thousand years. Three generations of Benito Concha's family prepare for the Eagle Dance. Benito says he sees the movements of the eagle as his teacher, and when he puts on eagle wings for the dance, he does so in honor and respect for that noble bird. Benito's performance is intercut with footage of eagles, and highlights the perfection of his movements.

Liang and the Magic Paintbrush

Written and illustrated by Demi
Henry Holt and Co., Inc.

In this enchanting old Chinese folk-tale, good and evil appear in a poor boy who is able to paint with magical results and the greedy emperor who does everything in his power to seize the boy's gift. Demi's watercolor art illuminates and enhances this tale of long ago, offering a glimpse of folklore from another culture.

Liang is a young working boy who earns money gathering firewood and cutting reeds. More than anything, however, he wishes to paint. But he cannot even afford to buy a brush. "One night as he slept an old man appeared as a phoenix and placed a brush in Liang's hand. 'It is a magic paintbrush. Use it carefully,' the old man said and flew away." Immediately, Liang begins to paint—and everything he paints comes to life. It is magic! When the greedy emperor hears of this, he demands that Liang and his paintbrush be captured. Just when the emperor thinks he has control of the gift, Liang outsmarts him by painting a picture so appealing, the emperor steps into it and is gone forever.

Program Description for
"Liang and the Magic Paintbrush"
(Show #107)

To get a feel for the sights, sounds, and tastes of Chinese culture, LeVar explores New York's Chinatown in "Liang and the Magic Paintbrush." An artist shares the beauty of Chinese calligraphy, writing "young friends" in flowing black characters. A special stamp is carved in soapstone for LeVar—it says "man who dwells in the rainbow."

Alex Wong serves LeVar a meal fit for an emperor—Grandma Wong's chicken soup, Mongolian beef, and candied bananas. LeVar joins in when the Lion Dance is performed, putting on the costume of one of the people dancing with the lion.

The Magic Wings: A Tale From China

By Diane Wolkstein
Illustrated by Robert Andrew Parker
E. P. Dutton, a division of Penguin Books USA Inc.

A Chinese girl yearns to sprout wings so that she may fly across the land and greet the coming of spring, in this Chinese folktale. Appropriately illustrated in Robert Andrew Parker's infamous wispy watercolor art, this is a wonderful book to read alone or to act out in a group.

A little Chinese girl spends her days tending geese in the hills for her aunt. When spring arrives, she wishes she could sprout wings and fly, like her geese, to greet the coming of spring. "Quickly she ran to the brook, and cupping some water in her hands, she wet her shoulders. Then she stood very straight in a sunny place and slowly began to flap her arms in the air." Others who see her selfishly want to be the first to sprout wings. "Soon all the girls and women were standing in a sunny place, flapping their arms in the air. Waiting . . ."

Finally, the Spirit in Heaven Who Grows Wings determines that one girl should be permitted to fly: "The goose girl felt a trembling behind her and a trembling all about her. A wind came and suddenly she was sailing in the air, higher and higher and higher. She saw crocuses and lilies, roses and lady slippers, violets and daisies, star grass and buttercups—The waiting was over. . . . 'Hello! Hello!' she called. . . . 'It's Spring!' "

Program Description for
"Bored—Nothing to Do!"
(Show #609)

(*The Magic Wings: A Tale From China* is a Review Book in this episode.)

LeVar explores the wild blue yonder in "Bored—Nothing to Do!" With a remote-controlled plane, he does loop-the-loops and nose dives and flies upside down. Using archival footage, a music video sings the praises of men and women who made the dream of flying come true.

Airports aren't all about flying, and a montage shows all the activity on the ground to get planes ready for their next flight. Then LeVar's cleared for takeoff, as he learns the ABC's of flying, from takeoff to landing. Book reviews include *Redbird*, which is read aloud by a blind boy who uses his fingers to read a Braille edition.

Mufaro's Beautiful Daughters

Written and illustrated by John Steptoe
Lothrop, Lee & Shepard Books

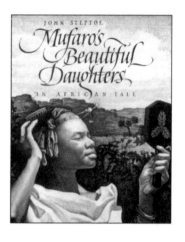

Reminiscent of Cinderella, this is the world-renowned African tale of two sisters, and their father, who would like one of them to become the king's bride. The magnificent illustrations by John Steptoe were inspired by the ruins of an ancient city found in Zimbabwe. The characters are named in the Shona language; Mufaro means "happy man," Nyasha means "mercy," Manyara means "ashamed," and Nyoko means "snake." The author has dedicated this stunning book to the children of South Africa.

When a messenger brings word that the king has asked for the most worthy and most beautiful daughter in the land to appear before him to choose as a wife, Mufaro orders his two beautiful daughters to go. But Manyara, the selfish one, steals ahead in the night, forsaking all kindness to creatures in the forest so that she will be first in line to meet the king. The next morning, Nyasha leaves, apprehensively, stopping on the way to help a snake, a little boy, and an old woman in need. When she reaches the kingdom, she finds that the king is a kind man with magic powers, who has been all of the creatures she helped (and that Manyara did not help), and Nyasha is asked to be his bride. Nyasha accepts his offer, and Manyara becomes a servant in the queen's household.

Program Description for
"Mufaro's Beautiful Daughters"
(Show #510)

"Mufaro's Beautiful Daughters" celebrates the music and culture of Africa. At a festival in New York's Central Park, LeVar meets Kimate Dinizulu, who shows him how to play many traditional African instruments, including those that are the ancient cousins of the trumpet and piano. Forces of Nature, a dance and music troupe, mixes old and new styles in a colorful and joyous performance of the LamKavenaBan Dance.

Viewers watch as an African drum maker uses a log to carve out a drum. First he shapes the instrument, then he scoops out the wood inside till it's hollow. The finishing touches are put on when he fastens the goatskin cover down with two "cradles." The drum maker says that so much of him goes into each instrument he creates that he feels that he shares the drum with the person who plays it.

The Paper Crane

Written and illustrated by Molly Bang
Greenwillow Books

This is a special book carrying the message that sometimes it is important to do something for nothing—the consequences may be very rewarding. In this ancient folktale magically retold by Molly Bang, one man's kindness brings another man good fortune. Illustrated in three-dimensional paper cutouts, this fine example of a children's picture book comes to life as the reader turns from one page to the next.

A local restaurant is very successful until a new highway is built, and then almost no one stops by to eat there anymore. One evening an unusual and gentle stranger, looking old and worn, comes to the restaurant and asks for food, even though he has no money. The owner invites him to sit down and enjoy a delicious meal. Afterward, the man picks up a paper napkin from the table and folds it into the shape of a crane. "You have only to clap your hands," he says, "and this bird will come to life and dance for you. Enjoy it while it is with you." With these words the stranger leaves. The owner does as he was told and the remarkable bird comes to life, immediately dancing!

Word of the dancing crane spreads, and people come from near and far to see the magic bird perform. Business booms and though the day comes when the old man takes the crane away, people still come, to hear stories of the gentle stranger and the magic crane made from a paper napkin.

Program Description for
"The Paper Crane"
(Show #409)

Japanese culture is celebrated in "The Paper Crane." Yoko Gates plays the koto, similar to a piano, and shows LeVar how she wears ivory picks on her fingertips to strum the strings. A chef carves delicate flowers and animals from vegetables such as white radishes, onions, and carrots.

Squares of paper become cranes, butterflies, and more in origami, the Japanese art of paper folding. An artist turns a pair of old blue jeans into a one-of-a-kind sheet of paper. The episode's finale is a performance by Japanese Festival Drummers—the fourteen men and women in the group are athletic musicians who spin around, trade places, and really bring the music to life.

Rainbow Crow

Retold by Nancy Van Laan
Illustrated by Beatriz Vidal
Alfred A. Knopf

Have you ever wondered why the crow has black feathers? This is the story of the Native American legend of long ago when the rainbow-colored crow's bravery saved all the forest creatures but consequently had an irreversible effect on the bird, even today. Beatriz Vidal's illustrations are brightly colored and eye-catching, reminiscent of primitive American art. Nancy Van Laan heard this beautiful story told by a Lenape elder, in Bucks County, Pennsylvania, and was inspired to adapt it for publication for a wider audience.

Before the two-legged walked the Earth, it was always warm. But one day, the Earth grew cold and tiny crystals drifted down from the sky. It was snowing. At first the animals were not afraid. But soon the snow became deeper, until some animals disappeared! They needed a messenger to travel to the Great Sky Spirit to ask him to stop the snow. Each animal refused the responsibility. "Suddenly, down from the top of the tallest tree, flew Rainbow Crow, the most beautiful bird on Earth, who called out to all the animals below in the sweetest voice of all birds. And he said: 'I will go. I will stop the snow.' "

For three days, Crow flew up to the sky, beyond the moon, stars, and clouds until he found the Great Sky Spirit. The Spirit explained that he could not stop the snow or the cold, but he could give Crow the gift of Fire, to stay warm and melt the snow until the spring weather returned. "The Great Spirit picked up a stick, put a bit of Fire on the end of it, and handed it to Crow." As he descended, sparks darkened his feathers, the stick burned shorter, and smoke and ash blowing into his mouth made his voice hoarse. "Caw, caw . . ."

In the forest, Crow flew close to the ground, melting the snow and saving his friends. All the animals thanked Crow and sang him praises. But still he wept—his rainbow feathers were gone forever. The Great Sky Spirit heard Crow and told him that soon the two-legged would appear on Earth and would take over the fire, and that Crow, for his bravery, would be granted the gift of freedom: Because of his smokey flavor, he would never be hunted. Because of his crackly voice, he would never be captured. " 'Your black feathers will shine. And they will reflect all the colors on Earth. If you look closely, you will see.' Then Crow looked, and he saw hundreds of tiny rainbows shining in his black feathers, and he was content."

Please refer to the program description for "The Legend of the Indian Paintbrush." *Rainbow Crow* **is a Review Book in this episode.**

Rumpelstiltskin

Retold and illustrated by Paul O. Zelinsky
E. P. Dutton, a division of Penguin Books USA Inc.

Here is a beautiful retelling of one of the brothers Grimm's most popular fairy tales. It is the story of how the miller's daughter, lovely and helpless, must outsmart the wretched Rumpelstiltskin, a little man who epitomizes greed. Paul O. Zelinsky's rich paintings, set in late medieval times, are truly magnificent. This version, far less gory than some other editions, makes an appropriate story in picture-book format to share with a new generation.

When a poor miller boasts to the king that his daughter can spin straw into gold, the king orders the girl to the castle, where he locks her in a room filled with straw. Weeping and distressed, the girl is relieved to find a tiny man enter and take on the task of spinning the straw into golden spools for her. A number of nights later, the girl has nothing left to offer the little man for his help. "Then promise that when you become queen, your first child will belong to me." Thinking she may never marry the king, she agrees.

Well, she does marry the king, and when she bears a son, the little man returns, demanding the child. The queen must find a way to relinquish her promise. Eventually, by guessing his name, she is left with family intact and the little man, Rumpelstiltskin, "jumped on his cooking spoon and flew out the window. And he never was heard from again."

Program Description for
"Rumpelstiltskin"
(Show #412)

LeVar journeys to the Renaissance Pleasure Fair in Agoura Hills, California, in "Rumpelstiltskin." It's like stepping back in time, as lords and ladies watch knights joust and everyone speaks the Queen's English—including Her Majesty herself, who addresses LeVar as "Sir LeVar of Burton."

A fair maid shows LeVar how she shears sheep and uses the wool to spin into threads. She dyes the yarn using the colored water made from boiling ground-up beet roots or madder tree bark for red and onion skin for yellow. Finally she weaves the threads on a loom; the whole process of making a garment takes about two weeks. LeVar gets caught in the cross fire between two jesting jugglers; feasts medieval-style, with no utensils; and is challenged to a duel—beanbags are the weapons of choice, and the loser gets dunked with water!

Why Mosquitoes Buzz in People's Ears

By Verna Aardema
Illustrated by Leo and Diane Dillon
Dial Books for Young Readers, a division of Penguin Books USA Inc.

An African "why" story, this is a stunning collaboration between author and illustrators that tells the tale of how mosquitoes came to have such an annoying buzz. Dense, colorful illustrations of the West African jungle enhance the onomatopoeic text. Storytellers will want to add this book to their repertoire, and children will find it riveting.

Iguana is offended by what Mosquito tells him, so he puts two sticks in his ears to save himself from any more nonsense. When Python says good morning to Iguana, Iguana doesn't hear him and ignores his friend. Python reads mischief into this and hides in Rabbit's hole, terrifying Rabbit and upsetting the whole forest. Because Mother Owl is upset, she does not hoot the sun into daylight and the forest remains dark.

Finally, King Lion calls all the creatures together and gets to the bottom of the problem. "Meanwhile the Mosquito had listened to it all from a nearby bush. She crept under a curly leaf, semm, and was never found and brought before the council. But because of this the mosquito has a guilty conscience. To this day she goes around whining in people's ears: 'Zeee! Is everyone still angry at me?' When she does that, she gets an honest answer. KPAO!"

Please refer to the program description for "The Gift of the Sacred Dog." *Why Mosquitoes Buzz in People's Ears* is a Review Book in this episode.

Family

Abuela

By Arthur Dorros
Illustrated by Elisa Kleven
Dutton Children's Books, a division of
Penguin Books USA Inc.

A little girl's confidence and imagination soar when she has her grandmother by her side for a day in New York City. The grandmother speaks only Spanish, and her words are translated with loving pride by her granddaughter Rosalba. This lovely, warm book introduces family love as well as Spanish culture and its beautiful language. The many sights the girl and her grandmother see are splendidly illustrated in a festival of color.

Rosalba and her grandmother Abuela take a remarkable trip—in Rosalba's imagination, when, during a bus ride, Rosalba begins to dream; what if she could fly? "*Ven*, Abuela. Come, Abuela," I'd say. "*Si, quiero volar*, Abuela would reply as she leaped into the sky with her skirt flapping in the wind. We would fly all over the city." Downtown, they would see the docked ships unload fruits "from the land where Abuela grew up. Mangos, bananas, papaya—those are all Spanish words."

Eventually, the two would become tired. "*Descansemos un momento*, Abuela would say. She wants to rest a moment. We would rest in our cloud chair, and Abuela would hold me in her arms, with the whole sky our house, *nuestra casa*." At the end of the day, it's back to street level and home until it's time for these inseparable companions to take their next adventure.

Please refer to the program description for "Mrs. Katz and Tush." *Abuela* **is a Review Book in this episode.**

A Chair for My Mother

Written and illustrated by Vera B. Williams
Greenwillow Books

In a story of recovery, a family finds that having a common goal can be inspirational, but having a family to share that goal with is the most comforting thing of all. Colorful illustrations, including border art, give full expression to this honest, tenderly written text.

A young girl lives with her mother and grandmother. Not so long ago they moved after a fire rampaged through their old apartment. Neighbors helped by bringing what they could, but what's really missing is an armchair. "When Mama comes home, her feet hurt. 'There's no good place for me to take a load off my feet,' she says. When Grandma wants to sit back and hum and cut up potatoes, she has to get as comfortable as she can on a hard kitchen chair. So that is how come Mama brought home the biggest jar she could find at the diner and all the coins started to go into the jar."

When the jar is finally full, it's time to go shopping. They find the chair they have all been dreaming of. They bring it home. The chair is as cozy and warm as the family that sits in it. "Now Grandma sits in it and talks with people going by in the daylight. Mama sits down and watches the news on TV when she comes home from her job. After supper, I sit with her and she can reach right up and turn out the light if I fall asleep in her lap."

Program Description for
"A Chair for My Mother"
(Show #20)

LeVar learns all about being a team player in "A Chair for My Mother." He and a group of dancers rehearse their routine, choreographed to a song called "Teamwork." The lyrics emphasize friends working together with friends. Throughout the show, the dancers practice their steps. The performance of "Teamwork" is the program's finale.

Viewers meet firefighters in training on a visit to the New York Fire Academy. On this close-knit team, each person has a specific job to do—including operating the hose and running the crane for a ladder rescue—and it can take two years to learn it all. Kids talk about what they do as a team that they can't do alone—like play hide and seek, sing in a chorus, and run a relay race.

Horace

Written and illustrated by Holly Keller
Greenwillow Books

This adoption story is about a child empowered to choose his parents, just as they have chosen him. Holly Keller's illustrations are sweet and unforgettable. The text is honest and depicts the incredible love that a family can have despite insecurities and in spite of differences. Anyone who has been welcomed to a second family will find particular comfort in reading this book.

Horace is a leopard in an adoptive tiger family. As much as he loves his mother and father, he feels funny because he has spots. All of his relatives have stripes. In an effort to look like them, "he tried to turn his spots into stripes [by connecting the dots], but it didn't work. Then he cut some pictures out of magazines [of spotted leopards] and hung them on the wall."

Still feeling strangely different, Horace goes to the park the next morning. Here he finds a big family, all spotted, like himself. He joins them and has a terrific time until it gets late. "The sun was going down and the air was chilly. Horace's feet felt cold. He thought about his slippers. He wondered if Papa was waiting for him to play checkers and if Mama missed him." Trekking on, he finds Mama and Papa looking for him and runs to their open arms. At bedtime that night, Mama tells him the story of his arrival, as she does every night. Afterward, Horace asks, "If you choose me, can I choose you, too?" "That would be very nice," Mama says. "Then I do, " Horace whispers, and he falls asleep.

Please refer to the program description for "Through Moon and Stars and Night Skies." *Horace* is a Review Book in this episode.

Little Nino's Pizzeria

Written and illustrated by Karen Barbour
Harcourt Brace

Is bigger always better? Not always, finds this family when they open up a new, bigger, better restaurant and leave behind the small pizzeria they once owned and loved. With all there is to do, the family discovers they miss what they enjoy the most—each other. Karen Barbour's easy-to-read text is highlighted by bold, appeal-ing, modern illustrations. The inspiration for this story came to her from a pizzeria she frequents in New York City.

"My dad, Nino, makes the best pizza in the world," says Tony. "I'm his best helper. People come from all over town to eat at Little Nino's. They wait in long lines because our restaurant is so small." One day, a man visits Nino and a new deal is struck. Little Nino's is closing, and soon Dad opens a big, fancy, expensive restaurant called Big Nino. "I asked my dad how I could help, but he was too busy to even notice me. No matter how I tried to be helpful, I was always in the way. So I went home."

Over time, Nino realizes that he misses making pizza and working with his family. He sells his big restaurant and reopens the old one. "But he changed the name of our restaurant. Little Tony's."

Program Description for
"Little Nino's Pizzeria"
(Show #603)

In "Little Nino's Pizzeria," LeVar gets more than he bargained for when he invites a few friends over for some homemade pizza and they end up inviting a whole basketball team! LeVar spends the day in the kitchen. Children talk about their favorite kind of pizza—and some of their tastes are out of this world.

"Little Nino's Pizzeria" serves as the inspiration to find out more about another family business—Fireworks by Grucci. Meet three generations of Gruccis working side by side as they set off one of the most dazzling fireworks displays in the country, New York City's Fourth of July celebration.

The Patchwork Quilt

By Valerie Flournoy
Illustrated by Jerry Pinkney
Dial Books for Young Readers, a division of Penguin Books USA Inc.

This book represents family love and closeness. Three generations work together to make a quilt for the youngest member of the household. Every inch of the quilt is hand-stitched during a difficult year, when Grandma is ill. Everyone pitches in and then finds great comfort when Grandma recovers and the quilt is completed. Jerry Pinkney's vibrant, full-color paintings exemplify the closeness that Valerie Flournoy's text describes.

When Grandma decides to make a quilt, young Tanya offers to help. Together, they collect scraps from any bits of leftover material or worn-out clothing they can find. "Sometimes the old ways are forgotten," Grandma says, as she sews by hand, but "a quilt won't forget. It can tell your life story." As the quilt gets bigger, Grandma becomes weaker, until she is bedridden. Her worried family takes up the quilt and continues to work on it. "Without saying a word Jim picked up the scissors and some scraps and started to make squares. Ted helped Jim put the squares in piles while Mama showed Tanya how to join them."

By springtime, Grandma feels much better, and one day, Tanya finds Grandma snipping the last thread to complete the masterpiece quilt. "Nobody had realized how big it had gotten. 'It's beautiful,' Papa said. He touched the gold patch, looked at Mama, and remembered. Jim remembered too. There was his blue and the red from Ted's shirt. There was Tanya's Halloween costume. And there was Grandma. Even though her patch was old, it fit right in."

Program Description for
"The Patchwork Quilt"
(Show #302)

Families and memories are the patches in "The Patchwork Quilt." LeVar joins a group of children making their very own quilt. Everyone talks about the special meaning their patch has—LeVar's is a picture of him sitting under a rainbow reading a book.

Viewers meet the Balducci family, who run a store full of tasty treats and dishes in New York City. Three generations of Balduccis work together—and everyone learns from grandfather, who tells them to take the time to do it right. A song about families is accompanied by beautiful photographs.

The Purple Coat

By Amy Hest
Illustrated by Amy Schwartz
Four Winds Press, a division of Macmillan Publishing Co.

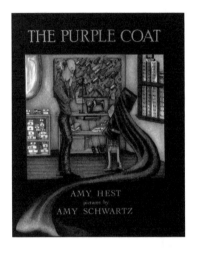

This delightful story offers the moral, sometimes it's good to try something new. When the familiar becomes humdrum and the feeling of change is in the air, go ahead—take the plunge. It will add some spice to your life and put some excitement in your day. Amy Schwartz has richly illustrated this story, giving full expression to the little girl and her immense desire to have a new purple coat to call her own.

Every fall, Gabby and her mother take two trains into the big city to visit Grandpa. Every fall, Grandpa, a tailor, sews Gabby a new navy blue coat. This year, Gabby would much prefer a purple coat! Purple?! Grandpa ponders this request. During lunch, he offers Gabby her choice of a salami or pastrami sandwich. "Salami," she answers, "the same as always." Grandpa asks "Want a bite of the leanest pastrami in town?" Gabby shakes her head. "I'll stick to what I know I like, salami." Grandpa then suggests that "once in a while it's good to try something new. How else do you know if you like it?"

After lunch, it's back to business. When Grandpa fingers the bolts of navy blue materials, Gabby reminds him of his own advice. Remembering that Gabby's mother had once yearned for a tangerine-colored dress—and received it—he agrees, announcing, "This year I will make you something very special, a coat that is navy blue on one side—and purple on the other. Reversible!" Gabby jumps high in the air. When she lands, her socks are scrunched around her ankles. "Let's make the purple side first," she exclaims. And they do.

Program Description for
"The Purple Coat"
(Show #505)

LeVar explores New York City's famed Garment District in "The Purple Coat." At the Fashion Institute of Technology, viewers meet young designers Julie Bliss and David Berg. At this school the final exam is a fashion show, and instead of a term paper, students sketch, cut out, and sew their own original designs. Some of the clothes are pretty outrageous, but as a montage shows, everyone has his own unique style.

In Kalamazoo, Michigan, sculptor Steve Hansen's style is to create humorous characters using papier-mâché, paint, and a lot of imagination. Viewers watch Steve transform one of his drawings into a three-dimensional figure that "looks back at you."

Three Days on a River in a Red Canoe

Written and illustrated by Vera B. Williams
Greenwillow Books

In this fun-filled guide, brimming with details for the outdoor lover in us all, take a three-day canoe trip down a winding river with the narrator of this book. Through the girl's diary, in composition-book format, we accompany her family as they purchase a canoe, map out the course, and actually paddle by day and sleep under the stars by night. Handy information such as knot tying and some delicious campfire recipes are included.

"I was the one who first noticed the red canoe for sale in a yard on the way home from school. My mom and my Aunt Rosie and my cousin Sam and I put our money together and bought it. The people who sold it to us threw in two paddles and two big old life jackets." So begins their journey, traveling from one beautiful spot to another, via canoe. The family learns to live with little more than just the basics and have a whole lot of fun in this lighthearted and informative adventure. From catching crayfish for dinner to jumping a waterfall, in sunny weather and cozy in the pouring rain, the group has a grand time and the reader is made to feel a part of it all from start to finish.

Program Description for
"Three Days on a River in a Red Canoe"
(Show #904)

The adaptation of *Three Days on a River in a Red Canoe* is broken into several parts, and is a mix of the original illustrations and photos of a dramatic reenactment of the story. LeVar goes camping with some friends and uses the feature book as a reference for camping and cooking tips. When night falls, they tell ghost stories around the campfire.

Over video footage of his vacation, LeVar tells about an exciting white-water rafting trip he took down the Zambezi River in Africa. He sees many wild animals, including baboons, crocodiles, and whooping cranes, but the wildest part of the journey occurs when he is swept overboard and rescued by helicopter!

Through Moon and Stars and Night Skies

By Ann Turner
Illustrated by James Graham Hale
A Charlotte Zolotow Book

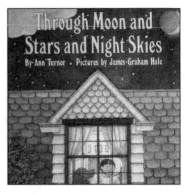

This is a most touching story about creating a family. In it, a young Asian boy remembers what it was like to fly a whole day and night to reach his adoptive momma and papa. He also recalls the photographs his new momma and papa send him that help to ease the transition. For the adoptive family, indeed any family, this book is a sincere, honest account of what it is like to receive the love and reassurance that a family, even a new one, can provide. Sensitive text and descriptive illustrations harmonize to make this an unforgettable reading experience.

The boy receives the pictures that his new momma and papa have sent. They show a man, a woman, and a red dog, a white house with a green tree out front, and a teddy-bear quilt on a bed— all waiting for him. The boy clutches these photos on the plane, never sleeping. At the airport, the boy meets the man and woman. As they introduce themselves and their home, the boy compares them with the photographs. They are the same!

That night, "Momma, you held out the teddy-bear quilt. I touched it. It was just like the picture. You lifted me into my new bed. You tucked the quilt around me. It was soft and warm. I knew that quilt. . . . I closed my eyes. I knew your voice now. I knew your smile. I was not so afraid anymore."

Program Description for
"Through Moon and Stars and Night Skies"
(Show #904)

There are all kinds of families, and "Through Moon and Stars and Night Skies" introduces viewers to three families brought together through adoption. Meet Cindy Peck, a single mom who opened her heart and home to nine Asian children; the Abneys, a family of four who adopted a dream girl named Tess; and the Harris family—Bill, Dorothy, Andrew, and Gavin. Ten-year-old Andrew sets the record straight for kids who think being adopted makes him weird: "I have a family, you have a family . . . we both have parents . . . what's the big deal?"

More kids and adults share the ups and downs of being fathers, mothers, sisters, brothers. And LeVar gets a surprise that he can really relate to. . . .

Tight Times

By Barbara Shook Hazen
Illustrated by Trina Schart Hyman
Viking Penguin, a division of Penguin Books USA Inc.

This is about a boy who is not allowed to get a dog. He does not understand what this means, but he knows it has something to do with eating lima beans instead of roast beef and having a baby-sitter after school since his mom has to work. Despite uncomfort-

able circumstances, when the boy finds a skinny little kitten outside on the street, his parents allow him to keep it and the boy is happy. Black-and-white illustrations portray the deep love this family feels for one another even though times are tough.

A young boy asks his father, "Why can't I have a dog? Last year you said I could have one when I was bigger. And I'm a lot bigger, see? So why not now? Because of tight times, said Daddy. He said I was too little to understand. I'm not too little, I said." The boy's father tries to explain that because they don't have enough money, they can't have all the things they would like.

A few days later, his father loses his job, and while his parents discuss it, the boy sits outside on their front step. He hears crying coming from a nearby garbage can. "There was something in there. It was a cat. I don't know how it got in but a nice lady helped me get it out. I never saw such a skinny little cat!"

The boy's parents allow him to keep the cat, and "after dinner Daddy asked me what I was going to call my cat. Dog, I said, because I always wanted one, even if I don't anymore." Despite their difficult situation, this family finds a way to share its love with one more, making home a little warmer place to be.

Program Description for
"Tight Times"
(Show #101)

In "Tight Times," all you need is a little imagination to have fun without spending a lot of money. The opportunities are endless: "rag basketball," coffee-can lid Frisbees, sock puppets, an old-fashioned game of tug-of-war, and more.

A music video called "Check It Out" has LeVar and friends dancing through the library, singing the praises of reading books. And kids show off their pets, including a seagull named Sweet Pea, Timmy the turtle, and pet rocks.

Fantasy

Gila Monsters Meet You at the Airport

By Marjorie Weinman Sharmat
Illustrated by Byron Barton
Macmillan Publishing Co.

This book was written for any child feeling anxious about a new experience. A little boy must move from New York City to "out West." He describes, in the first person, exactly why he would prefer to stay put. With perception and a keen sense of the ridiculous, this author-illustrator team has created a very funny book that never loses compassion for the child who fears the unknown.

The boy in this story has a wild imagination and may have seen one too many old cowboy movies. His preconceived ideas about life out West make him feel apprehensive about leaving New York. "My mother and father are moving. Out West. They say I have to go, too. They say I can't stay here forever." The boy explains many of the reasons he would like to stay forever. "Out West it takes fifteen minutes just to say hello. Like this: H-O-W-W-W-D-Y, P-A-A-A-R-D-N-E-R." Out West, he'll have to wear chaps and spurs and ride a horse to school each day, and he doesn't know how. Out West, huge lizards meet you at the airport. Out West, he'll have to eat chili and beans for breakfast, lunch, and dinner, and he'll miss his friend Seymour.

The airplane lands. No gila monsters. The family drives to their new home (in a taxi, not on horseback) and along the way the boy doesn't see *one* buffalo stampede. Children in the neighborhood look like him! His new home looks okay too. Reassured, the boy walks into his house saying, "Tomorrow I'm writing a long letter to Seymour. I'll tell him I'm sending it by pony express. Seymour will believe me. Back East they don't know much about us Westerners."

Program Description for
"Gila Monsters Meet You at the Airport"
(Show #108)

Moving to a new place, mysterious gila monsters, and misconceptions about desert life are all explored in "Gila Monsters Meet You at the Airport." Kids guess at what a gila monster really is, then viewers get a chance to meet one! A biologist in Arizona shows it's not very monstrous after all, only about a foot and a half long.

A music video called "Used to Think" mixes illustrations from the book and footage of Arizona to tell the true story of the Wild West. LeVar talks to a group of children who share their thoughts on changing schools and moving to new places.

Jumanji
Written and illustrated by Chris Van Allsburg
Houghton Mifflin Co.

Sometimes the consequences of finders keepers losers weepers are not always pleasant, as seen in this wildly imaginative and nonsensical story, where two unsupervised children get more than they bargained for when they play a new game in their living room. In his eminent style, renowned author-illustrator Chris Van Allsburg has created a tale that will hold children spellbound.

When two youngsters are left alone by their parents one afternoon, they decide to end their boredom with a walk in the park. Once there, they find an abandoned board game and excitedly bring it home. Judy reads, "Jumanji, a young people's jungle adventure especially designed for the bored and restless . . . VERY IMPORTANT: ONCE A GAME OF JUMANJI IS STARTED IT WILL NOT BE OVER UNTIL ONE PLAYER REACHES THE GOLDEN CITY."

The directions do not seem out of the ordinary, but when Peter rolls the dice and reads, "Lion attacks, move back 2 spaces," he and his sister are *very* surprised to find a fierce, *real* lion next to them! With the next roll, two *real* monkeys appear and wreak havoc in the kitchen! Followed by a monsoon, flooding, and even a herd of rhinoceroses, the children play as fast as they can, hoping to end this game and this bizarre day. When Judy finally wins and cries out, "Jumanji!" suddenly everything clears and is just as it was before the game. Bolting out the door, the two run back to the park and leave the game where they found it. When their parents arrive home, their mother asks, "Did you have an exciting afternoon?"

Program Description for
"Brush"
(Show #504)

(*Jumanji* is a Review Book in this episode.)

An ordinary brush comes to life and becomes a family's prized pet in the book adaptation in "Brush." LeVar explores the warehouse where all the floats and balloons are kept for the Macy's Thanksgiving Day Parade. It takes a lot of work to bring the parade creatures to life—six people operate the trademark turkey float alone. Viewers watch a Snoopy balloon go from the drawing board to inflation.

At the hands of 3-D animators Rob and Becky, anything can happen—objects on a kitchen table spin to life; a frog pedals a unicycle; and a dino-mite book sprouts legs, arms, and a head to become a book-a-saurus. Puppet master Kevin Clash makes viewers see double—two LeVars! LeVar and his puppet twin close the show together.

The Runaway Duck
Written and illustrated by David Lyon
Lothrop, Lee & Shepard Books

Readers will learn to expect the unexpected in this silly, very witty story about a pull-toy duck's adventures as he travels around the world, helpless but seemingly determined to find his owner. The art is unique, and Egbert, the duck, is unflappably funny as he follows an uncharted course over land, sea, and air.

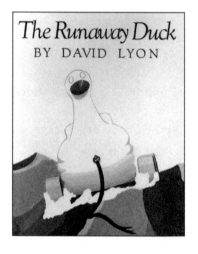

"Egbert was a carved wooden duck with wheels and a long nylon string for pulling. The wheels were mounted on metal axles and rolled very smoothly. One wheel had a plaque on which Sebastian had written his name." When he's called in from the garage for lunch, Sebastain ties Egbert to the bumper of his father's car so that he won't roll away. After lunch, Sebastian's father drives away on a long business trip, and "by the time Sebastian remembered, Egbert was doing sixty miles an hour down Route 95."

A sharp mountain turn breaks Egbert's string and sends him flying—almost like a real duck—until he falls into a stream. The stream opens up into the ocean, where Egbert is tossed about unmercifully and winds up, missing his special wheel, on a deserted island. A shipwrecked Frenchman named Jacques finds him. All the while, Sebastian worries about his beloved Egbert. Where can he be?

Eventually, Jacques and Egbert are saved and make headline news in the local French newspaper. Sebastian sees their picture and finally regains his favorite toy. Egbert looks a little worse for wear, but wheel or no wheel, it's definitely him. A missing toy never had such an adventure as Egbert, the runaway duck.

Program Description for
"The Runaway Duck"
(Show #410)

Everything is just ducky in "The Runaway Duck." LeVar spends the day on Chesapeake Bay to learn more about these "fowl" creatures. Vidal Martinez, of the Blackwater Wildlife Refuge, tells LeVar the difference between ducks and geese. Kids demonstrate how they would call ducks—including, "Get over here, duck!"

Experienced duck callers strut their stuff, showing there's more than one way to call a duck. Artists Ed and Ester Burns turn a block of wood into a beautifully detailed model of a duck. Ed carves the wood and burns in the intricate patterns of the feathers; then it's Ester's turn, and she paints the model and puts on the finishing touches.

Friendship

Frog and Toad Together
Written and illustrated by Arnold Lobel
HarperCollins

In this I Can Read chapter book, there
are five delightful stories about two
inseparable best friends named Frog
and Toad, who find that life is full of
fun, always interesting, and often
funny when there's someone to share
it with. Arnold Lobel's illustrations
(including one of the two playing
leapfrog) are charming and wholesome. This is one of four irresistible
books about Frog and Toad.

In one story, Toad has baked cookies. They are so good that he
runs to Frog's house and together they begin eating one delicious
cookie after another. "We need willpower," says Frog. So they hide
the cookies in a box tied with string, up a ladder, on a high shelf.
"But we can climb the ladder and take the box down from the shelf
and cut the string and open the box," says Toad. They retrieve the
box and offer all of the cookies to the birds outside. Proudly, Frog
announces that they, indeed, have lots of willpower. "You may

keep it all, Frog," says Toad. "I am going home now to bake a cake."

In another story, Toad has had a bad dream. He wakes in the morning to find Frog standing near his bed. " 'Frog,' he said, 'I am so glad that you came over.' 'I always do,' said Frog. Then Frog and Toad ate a big breakfast, and after that they spent a fine, long day together." These characters are sensitive and inclusive. The reader will be welcomed by Frog and Toad on their adventures, no matter what the day has in store.

Program Description for
"Three by the Sea"
(Show #411)

(*Frog and Toad Together* is a Review Book in this episode.)

The book adaptation "Three by the Sea" is about a trio of friends and the tales they tell each other one day. LeVar goes seaside and finds people storytelling in the sand, sculpting animals into the beach.

Improvisational comedy troupe Chicago City Limits do a different kind of storytelling: they act out scenes in which kids' dreams come true. A boy becomes a star football player, a girl a tap dancer, and troupe members act out the roles of their entourages: manager, coach, agent, parent. A music video shows how friends can work together to make their very own storybook.

Mrs. Katz and Tush

Written and illustrated by Patricia Polacco
A Bantam Little Rooster Book

Friendships that recognize differences and celebrate likenesses can often be the strongest. In this tender story, an intergenerational, interracial friendship between a lonely Jewish widow and a young African-American boy develops when an abandoned kitten needs a home. Together, they find similarities in each other's heritage worth sharing and overcoming, and separately, they know that each is a unique individ-

ual. Expressive artwork and lively dialogue make this subtle story come alive with meaning.

When kittens were born in the basement of Larnel's apartment building, he decides to give the last one to lonely Mrs. Katz. Hesitantly, she agrees to take the kitten if Larnel will come over to help. "Larnel kept his promise. He visited Mrs. Katz and Tush every day after school. There was always a fresh-baked kugel and a tall glass of milk waiting for him. But as much as he grew to love Tush, he also loved to listen to Mrs. Katz talk about the old country and the way times used to be." During their many conversations, they learn that they have much in common. "Larnel, your people and mine are alike, you know. Trouble, we've seen. Happiness, too. Great strength we've had. You and I are alike, so much alike!"

Time passes and their friendship deepens. Larnel helps Mrs. Katz find Tush when Tush has escaped through an open window. He joins Mrs. Katz for Passover seder, and shares in the joy when Tush delivers four beautiful kittens. "As the years passed, Mrs. Katz, Tush and her descendants became part of Larnel's family. There were graduations, weddings, new babies, and finally a kaddish." The friendship between Larnel and Mrs. Katz lives on in these memorable pages from which children will grow and benefit with every reading.

Program Description for
"Mrs. Katz and Tush"
(Show #908)

Friendships between young and old are the heart of "Mrs. Katz and Tush." LeVar strolls down a lively street, meeting friends and neighbors along the way. He stops by for a visit with Sherry, his very own "Mrs. Katz." Sherry teaches LeVar how to make challah bread, potato latkes, and matzoh balls. She explains the significance of these foods for Jewish people.

Children share stories about grandparents and other older friends and role models. A music video weaves together a wonderful song and beautiful pictures of relationships that cross generations. This show is sure to tug at your heartstrings.

Wilfrid Gordon McDonald Partridge

By Mem Fox
Illustrated by Julie Vivas
American edition by Kane/Miller

Wilfrid Gordon McDonald Partridge
Written by Mem Fox   Illustrated by Julie Vivas

In this book a little boy tries to find the meaning of "memory" so that he can help out an elderly friend. Charming text and unique illustrations show the importance of intergenerational friendships, without which, the young do not grow old and the old do not stay young.

"There was once a small boy called Wilfrid Gordon McDonald Partridge and what's more he wasn't very old either. His house was next door to an old people's home and he knew all the people who lived there." Wilfrid Gordon was friends with Mrs. Jordan, Mr. Hosking, Mr. Tippett, Miss Mitchell, and Mr. Drysdale, "but his favorite person of all was Miss Nancy Alison Delacourt Cooper because she had four names just as he did. He called her Miss Nancy and told her all his secrets."

One day, Wilfrid Gordon overhears his parents say that poor Miss Nancy, at ninety-six, has lost her memory. So he goes to all his friends at the home asking what a memory is. He learns that it is something warm, from long ago, that makes you cry, that makes you laugh, and is something precious as gold. "So Wilfrid Gordon went home again to look for memories for Miss Nancy because she had lost her own."

He collects shells (he had found long ago), a puppet on a string (that made everyone laugh), a medal (from his grandfather), his football (precious as gold), and an egg fresh (and warm) from the henhouse. "Then Wilfrid Gordon called on Miss Nancy and gave her each thing one by one. 'What a dear, strange child to bring me all these wonderful things,' thought Miss Nancy. Then she started to remember . . . and the two of them smiled and smiled because Miss Nancy's memory had been found again by a small boy, who wasn't very old either."

Please refer to program description for "Mrs. Katz and Tush." *Wilfrid Gordon McDonald Partridge* **is a Review Book in this episode.**

History

Follow the Drinking Gourd

Written and illustrated by Jeanette Winter
Alfred A. Knopf

During the early days of slavery in the United States, many slaves tried to escape their unjust bondage by fleeing north—to Canada usually—to find freedom. By the 1840s a group of slaves, free blacks, and white sympathizers had formed a secret network comprised of places for slaves to hide

and people to help them while on this dangerous journey to freedom. This network came to be called the Underground Railroad. One of the "conductors," a one-legged sailor named Peg Leg Joe, is highlighted in this story, based on fact, in which we come to know the meaning of his song "Follow the Drinking Gourd."

This folk song, sung by slaves, sounded very simple but actually it was a map to freedom, for hidden in its lyrics were directions to the Underground Railroad trail. "When the sun comes back, and the first quail calls [spring arrives], follow the drinking gourd [Big Dipper]. For the old man is a-waiting for to carry you to freedom

[Peg Leg Joe on a boat to take runaways across the Ohio River to Canada] if you follow the drinking gourd." Art in the style of traditional American folk paintings illustrates this historical song as Peg Leg Joe helps one family find its way to freedom.

Program Description for
"Follow the Drinking Gourd"
(Show #1001)

"Follow the Drinking Gourd" takes LeVar to South Carolina, where he brings us through an old slave ship and onto a plantation to see how slaves lived. LeVar explains what life was like for Africans who were brought to this country against their will. Dramatic reenactments further show what life was like then, and why people risked their lives running away from the plantations.

Members of the musical group Sweet Honey in the Rock sing the history of African Americans and explain how the past affects their music. Using just their voices, the women of Sweet Honey make incredibly powerful music.

If You Are a Hunter of Fossils

By Byrd Baylor
Illustrated by Peter Parnall
Charles Scribner's Sons

In this inspiring introduction to pale-ontology, science is poetry as a fossil hunter searches for signs of the past in western Texas. Flowing, thought-ful text and desert-filled illustrations will offer the reader visions of fossils and their imprints on the rocks that have been here for so many millions of years. The present holds the key to our past in this exquisite picture book.

A woman speaks gently about her calling in life. "Maybe you are a hunter of fossils—like me. I am the one on the side of the West Texas mountain reading the rock looking for signs of the sea that was here." As she finds fossils from the past, she proudly explains what it feels like to hold history at her fingertips. "Up here, what's *real* is the shallow warm Cretaceous sea that all those seashells knew. On this mountain every rock still holds the memory of that time. When you are here, you hold it too."

See history come alive as the fossil hunter describes the incredibly slow process, taking millions of years, of our ocean turn-ing to stone. "Now that sea is a mountain of rock that I climb with a shell in my hand." Take the time to slow down and savor this very personal book.

Please refer to the program description for "Digging Up Dinosaurs." *If You Are a Hunter of Fossils* is a Review Book in this episode.

Mummies Made in Egypt
Written and illustrated by Aliki
HarperCollins

In this extremely informative account, Aliki explains the ancient Egyptian technique of mummification and the reasons for its use. The process is described with straightforward text, detailed illustrations, and sidebar highlights. Children will find their preconceived ideas about mummies dispelled and the reality of the approach fascinating. Many of Aliki's illustrations are adapted from paintings and sculptures found in ancient Egyptian tombs.

In the desert of ancient Egypt, beyond the Nile River, the ancient Egyptians buried their dead. But how did they do it? And why? "Egyptians believed that after they died a new life began." With their "ba," or soul, and "ka," an invisible twin, they could travel from the body to the other world and keep in contact with those they left behind. "In order for a person to live forever, the ba and ka had to be able to recognize the body, or they could not return to it. This is why the body had to be preserved, or mummified."

The process took place over a period of seventy days, from the embalming bed, where the corpse was drained, bejeweled, and bound, to the coffin, sarcophagus, and tomb which held the body. If a person was a rich pharaoh (a king in Egypt), he would be buried in a great pyramid which took hundreds of workers their lifetime to build. Once buried, "the mummy was in its eternal rest-ing place and on the way to its new life." Through the use of X-ray machines, now, thousands of years later, scientists have found many of these mummies perfectly preserved, just as the ancient Egyptians planned.

Program Description for
"Mummies Made in Egypt"
(Show #509)

In "Mummies Made in Egypt" a camel carries LeVar to the Museum of Fine Arts in Boston for a close-up look at Egyptian mummies. Luckily, he finds space at the "Camel Parking" meter out in front. But LeVar's out of luck at the end of the show when time runs out on the meter, and a policeman gives him a ticket!

In the museum, LeVar explains that by examining the pictures on the sarcophagus of a mummy named Ta-Bess, scientists know that she was a singer in the choir and married to a barber. In Kalamazoo, Michigan, another ancient mummy is rushed to the hospital in an ambulance—for a CT scan that will reveal what's been under wraps for over four thousand years. A forensic artist uses the X-rays as a blueprint to create an exact 3-D replica of the mummy's head. When he's done, viewers see a face that's been hidden for centuries.

The Ox-Cart Man

By Donald Hall
Illustrated by Barbara Cooney
Viking Penguin, a division of
Penguin Books USA Inc.

American life during the early 1800s is depicted as a farmer and his family prepare all year to sell their goods at the annual Portsmouth Market. Gently told, the story comes full circle after everything is sold successfully and the resourceful family begins again for the next year. This glimpse into a time gone by is magnificently illustrated in a special medium that resembles early American wood paintings.

"In October he backed his ox into his cart and he and his family filled it up with everything they made or grew all year long that was left over." His wife has woven shawls from their sheared sheep. His daughter has knit mittens out of yarn spun from the sheep's wool. His son has made birch brooms, and the ox-cart man has split shingles from trees off their land.

The farmer brings these and many other goods to the bustling market in Portsmouth. All the goods are sold. "Then he sold his ox, and kissed him good-bye on his nose." With his pockets full of coins, he buys necessary items and two pounds of wintergreen peppermint candies for his family and walks home, arriving just in time for a delicious supper before starting a new day.

Program Description for
"The Ox-Cart Man"
(Show #203)

In "The Ox-Cart Man," LeVar heads for Old Sturbridge Village in Massachusetts for a look at life in nineteenth-century America. The people who work there learn about history by living it. Viewers watch two young oxen learn how to work as a team in a yoke, heeding commands like "gee" and "ha."

In the kitchen, LeVar finds some interesting contraptions not used today—kids guess the use of one gadget sure to toast your tootsies. LeVar lends a helping hand to the village blacksmith and learns the origin of the saying "Strike while the iron is hot." A good old-fashioned dance closes the show.

A River Ran Wild

Written and illustrated by Lynne Cherry
Gulliver Books/Harcourt Brace

The environmental history of the Nashua River, flowing between New Hampshire and Massachusetts, its destruction and remarkable recovery, is told with accuracy and spirit in this inspiring ecological story. Overpopulation and man's industrial revolution claimed the river, leaving it for dead, until one grassroots organization decided to take matters into its own hands. Border illustrations enhance the detailed text and will stimulate further discussion of our natural resources and what we can do to restore them.

Records of the Nashua River date back to as early as the 1300s, when Native Americans settled there. The Nashua Indian people called the river Nash-a-way—River with the Pebbled Bottom—because of its sparklingly clear water. As centuries went by, more and more people settled there, building homes and factories. "These were times of much excitement, times of 'progress' and 'invention.' Factories along the Nashua River made new things of new materials. Telephones and radios and other things were created from plastics. Chemicals and plastic waste were also dumped into the river. Soon the Nashua's fish and wildlife grew sick from this pollution." Until, by the 1960s, millions of gallons of raw sewage and waste were being dumped directly into the river.

Inspired by a descendant of the early settlers, a woman named Marion Stoddart started the Nashua River Clean Up Committee. Her commitment evoked many people's support. "They signed petitions and sent letters. They protested to politicians and showed them jars of dirty water. They convinced the paper mills to build a plant to process the waste. They persuaded the factories to stop dumping. Finally new laws were passed and the factories stopped polluting." Presently this river runs wild. Animals stop to drink the water, and humans are proud to be living near such a beautiful river. With the abundance of environmental issues facing children today, this picture book will teach the younger generation much about the world in which they live.

Program Description for
"And Still the Turtle Watched"
(Show #1004)

(*A River Ran Wild* is a Review Book in this episode.)

We can all take action to protect and preserve the environment— this is the message of the episode "And Still the Turtle Watched." Meet New York schoolchildren who are planting trees not only to make their neighborhood more beautiful, but also so there will be more oxygen for us all to breathe. And listen to these children sing a song to the environment, "You Mean the World to Us."

Travel across the country to Oklahoma, home of the Sutton Avian Research Center. They sponsor a number of programs to help endangered birds, including the bald eagle. Efforts to save our national bird are followed, as Sutton team members take eagle eggs under their wing to ensure the birds survive and can repopulate areas where the bald eagle has disappeared.

Sunken Treasure

Written and illustrated by Gail Gibbons
HarperCollins

Gail Gibbons, master of picture-book nonfiction, tells in graphic detail the story of the seventeenth-century Spanish galleon *Nuestra Señora de Atocha*, which sank in 1622, carrying gold, jewels, silver bars, and thousands of coins. Its salvage by Mel Fisher and his crew proves to be the richest such treasure ever found. Details of the search and the find are accounted for, offering a glimpse of life long ago. In this book, history comes alive.

In 1622 the *Atocha*, laden with riches, is caught in a hurricane off the coast of Florida. The hull breaks open and she sinks. Spain wants its treasures back, but the *Atocha* cannot be found. Centuries later, in the early 1960s, a new search begins. A man named Mel Fisher is determined to find the lost treasure ship. With boats, crew, equipment, and investors to support his mission, he sets out to find the galleon. In 1971 they discover a silver bar with markings to match the *Atocha*'s, proof that they have found the treasure. Then, in 1985, the mother lode is discovered. "Mel Fisher's twenty-year search is finally over. Resting on the ocean floor, 55 feet below, is the *Atocha*'s fabled treasure—glinting gold bars, jewelry, gold and silver coins, and other precious finds. Nearly all the listed cargo is there, and more—some treasure must have been smuggled aboard."

Each piece of treasure must be accounted for. Everything is marked on a grid, sketched, and photographed before being lifted. The salvage goes on for weeks, months, and years. The treasures of the *Nuestra Señora de Atocha*, worth hundreds of millions of dollars, are brought to a building back on the mainland to be cleaned, catalogued, and displayed to the public. "The wreck and its artifacts will be studied by historians and archaeologists for years to come. Their discoveries will enrich our knowledge of the past. This will be the second treasure of the *Atocha*." Dive into this true adventure where giving up is out of the question.

Program Description for
"Sunken Treasure"
(Show #705)

Actual footage of the *Atocha* treasure hunt brings the book to life in "Sunken Treasure." LeVar hits the beach at Pirate's Cove looking for riches buried in the sand by Dogtooth Louie. After searching without luck, LeVar gets a little help from a bloodhound named Baskerville. But the treasure isn't what he expected, and as LeVar finally clues in to what Dogtooth meant, Baskerville enjoys the riches.

Viewers meet Dr. Robert Ballard, of the Woods Hole Oceanographic Institute in Massachusetts, a scientist and treasure hunter who located and explored the most famous shipwreck in history—the *Titanic*. Using a robot named Jason Junior and a minisubmarine known as *Alvin*, Ballard films inside the wreck, revealing a ghostly world unseen for over seventy years.

Wagon Wheels

By Barbara Brenner
Illustrated by Don Bolognese
Harper

Wagon Wheels documents a fascinating slice of time in African-American history. In the year 1878, Ed Muldie and his family left Kentucky to settle in Kansas. The Homestead Act, promising free land to anyone willing to settle in the West, was an opportunity not to be missed now that African Americans were offered the freedom they so long deserved. The words of an eleven-year-old boy are richly illustrated to help the reader actually imagine what life was like in Kansas in the 1870s. This story is based on fact.

In this I Can Read chapter book, the Muldies arrive in Nicodemus, Kansas. Without their mother, who died during the journey, they build a dugout home and must survive the bitter winter. "It wasn't much of a place—dirt floor, dirt walls, no windows. And the roof was just grass and branches. But we were glad to have this dugout when the wind began to whistle across the prairie."

The three sons, ages eleven, eight, and three, must endure their father's absence, in the dugout, while he continues the search for the proper land to call home. When word finally comes of his settlement, the boys travel, alone, for twenty-two days to find him. This is a gripping adventure story that will have the reader cheering when the strong-willed boys are finally reunited with their father.

Please refer to the program description for "The Ox-Cart Man." *Wagon Wheels* **is a Review Book in this episode.**

The Wall

By Eve Bunting
Illustrated by Ronald Himler
Clarion Books: A Houghton Mifflin Co.
imprint

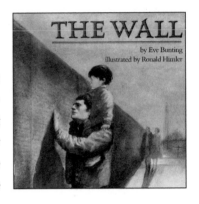

This picture book serves as a tribute to the Vietnam Veterans Memorial, located in Washington, D.C. Restrained text and moving illustrations tell the story of a boy and his father coming to the wall, from far away, to find the name of the boy's grandfather. It is appropriate to read this book along with a child, particularly on Memorial Day or whenever war and its consequences are being discussed.

"This is the wall, my grandfather's wall. On it are the names of those killed in a war, long ago. . . . The wall is black and shiny as a mirror. In it I can see Dad and me. I can see the bare trees behind us and the dark, flying clouds." Together, the boy and his father look for Grandpa's name. "Dad runs his fingers along the rows of print and I do, too. The letters march side by side, like rows of soldiers. They're nice and even. It's better printing than I can do. The wall is warm."

They finally find Grandpa's name, GEORGE MUNOZ. They make a rubbing of the name and Dad puts the paper in his wallet. Out of his wallet, he slides a picture. The boy places the picture of himself under his grandfather's name. "It's sad here," says the boy. His father puts his hand on his son's shoulder. "I know. But it's a place of honor. I'm proud that your grandfather's name is on this wall." "I am too," says the boy. This book has a tremendous impact on all who read it.

Program Description for
"The Wall"
(Show #807)

Walls that bring people together instead of separating them are featured in "The Wall." LeVar visits the Vietnam Veterans Memorial in Washington D.C., better known simply as the Wall. Its creator, architect Maya Lin, explains her goals in designing the memorial—she wanted something that people would respond to, and since names evoke the most meaning, she focused on them. The Wall is low to the ground so that as you go down, the names rise above you. Creating a memorial is like talking across time, says Maya Lin; the important thing isn't to glorify war, but to honor the people who were there.

Striking archival footage shows the faces of George Washington, Thomas Jefferson, Theodore Roosevelt, and Abraham Lincoln being blasted into the granite cliff walls at Mount Rushmore. Ninety percent of the sculpture was done this way, using precise amounts of dynamite to blow away exact pieces of rock. Artist Juan Sanchez paints a mural honoring jazz musician Louis Armstrong, using a grid system to transfer the painting from his sketch pad to the enormous wall.

Humor

Cloudy With a Chance of Meatballs
By Judi Barrett
Illustrated by Ron Barrett
Atheneum Publishers, an imprint of Macmillan Publishing Co.

You may have heard of it raining cats and dogs but how about spaghetti and meatballs? Enjoy a fantasy come true by reading about the town of Chewand-swallow, where no one ever has to go food shopping because their meals materialize from the sky. The reader will laugh out loud when the weather takes a turn for the worse and things get out of hand. The mayhem is captured in bold pen-and-ink illustrations, laced with subtle innuendos that add greatly to this bizarre story. Children will literally be hungry for more after they have a taste of this book.

The people in Chewandswallow lead a delicious life. Three times a day, the sky opens up and a meal rains, snows, or storms in. "Dinner one night consisted of lamb chops becoming heavy at times, with occasional ketchup. Periods of peas and baked potatoes were followed by gradual clearing, with a wonderful Jell-O setting in the west." One day the weather takes a turn for the worse and the people find their meals growing larger in proportion *and* size.

The townspeople fear for their lives as giant doughnuts and downpours of maple syrup hit the town. "So a decision was made to abandon the town of Chewandswallow. It was a matter of survival." Gluing together giant pieces of stale bread with peanut butter, each person sets sail for a new land. They find a nice coastal town and use their stale bread to build houses. They settle there and are happy, although buying food at a grocery store takes some getting used to.

Please refer to the program description for "June 29, 1999." *Cloudy With a Chance of Meatballs* **is a Review Book in this episode.**

The Day Jimmy's Boa Ate the Wash

By Trinka Hakes Noble
Illustrated by Steven Kellogg
Dial Books for Young Readers, a division of Penguin Books USA Inc.

In this very silly, cumulative tale, a class trip to the farm turns out to be anything but dull when young Jimmy brings his pet boa constrictor along! The snake wreaks havoc on farm, farmer, and fowl, much to the children's delight. Steven Kellogg's wonderful illustrations capture the moment, as seen in the animals' zany actions, the children's gleeful reactions, and the look of surprise on Mother's face when Jimmy's classmate recounts the day's chain of events.

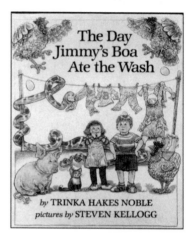

Told by a girl in Jimmy's class, the story begins innocently enough. The trip is ordinary, kind of dull even, until the cow starts crying. A cow crying? Well, yes, because a haystack falls on her. What? A haystack falls because the farmer, yelling at the pigs, crashes into it with his tractor! Why, what are the pigs doing? The pigs are on the school bus eating everyone's lunch! On it goes until it is finally discovered that Jimmy has brought along his pet boa constrictor—to meet the animals! Needless to say, the animals are not pleased by the introduction.

Great fun is had by the children as they follow the boa everywhere the snake goes, causing mishap after mishap. See for yourself what a crazy day it can be when Jimmy brings his boa along for a day at the farm!

Program Description for
"The Day Jimmy's Boa Ate the Wash"
(Show #144)

Animals of all kinds populate "The Day Jimmy's Boa Ate the Wash." LeVar has an unusual day when he meets a tarantula and a snake named Fang. An animated cartoon speculates about the funny things that could happen if a boa constrictor followed LeVar to the livestock show.

Two farm girls talk about why they think pigs make better pets than dogs. A bouncy song pays tribute to that henhouse specialty, the egg. And at the livestock show, people and their sheep are on display when judges must decide who's the best.

Duncan and Dolores

by Barbara Samuels
Bradbury Press, an affiliate of Macmillan Publishing Co.

This book will have special meaning for every child who has been shunned by a family pet. In it, a little girl adopts a mature cat and must learn that smothering him with attention is not necessarily the way to win his heart. When her older sister steps in and offers some gentle advice, the table turns and suddenly everyone gets along better than expected. This story is funny, warm, and fast-paced and the discreet message it sends is one to which every beginning reader can relate.

When Dolores sees the sign offering Duncan, a four-year-old cat, for adoption, she knows what she wants. "He's cute . . . and he's just my age. I want a cat like that." Faye, her sister, reminds Dolores that animals run away from her, but that doesn't discourage Dolores. The next day, Duncan arrives, and for a while Dolores tries to force him to play, dress up, and do tricks—to no avail. Finally Faye suggests that Duncan may be afraid of Dolores and that she should leave him alone. Dolores responds, "Duncan afraid of me, how silly! YOU'RE NOT AFRAID OF ME, ARE YOU, DUNCAN?" Duncan has cleared the room.

Despite her skepticism, Dolores takes her sister's advice and plays in her hiding place alone, has a tea party with her dolls and does not invite Duncan, and when it's nap time, she hugs her teddy bear, not Duncan. Later that day, Duncan begins to vie for Dolores's attention, and that night, he even sleeps on her bed. Needless to say, Dolores is thrilled, bursting to her sister, "DUNCAN REALLY LIKES ME!" The last illustration shows Dolores hanging over her bed looking at the tip of Duncan's tail peeking out from under the bed. Oh well, things may not change overnight, but the reader will see that exercising patience can mean progress, resulting in the comfort of unconditional love.

Program Description for
"Duncan and Dolores"
(Show #507)

Here, kitty kitty! Cats of all shapes and sizes are spotlighted in "Duncan and Dolores." At Marine World in Vallejo, California, LeVar meets a purr-fect cat—a beautiful full-grown Bengal tiger. Trainer Peter Gross translates tiger talk, explaining that big cats purr too. In the newborn nursery, baby tigers—so blond their stripes barely show—are taught their manners. Trainers romp with the adult tigers, jumping, splashing in the pool, and nuzzling.

Viewers go backstage for a glimpse into the secret world of the musical *Cats*. Using photos of real cats for reference, the actress who plays Grizabella transforms herself into a glamour cat with the careful use of makeup called greasepaint. Then it's showtime—and Grizabella sings the showstopper "Memory."

Florence and Eric Take the Cake

Written and illustrated by Jocelyn Wild
Dial Books for Young Readers, a division of
Penguin Books USA Inc.

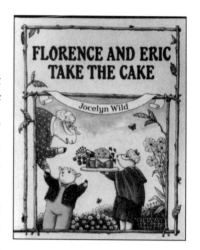

This is a delightfully silly story that captures the irony and hysteria of good intentions gone wrong. Two young lambs mistake a hat for a cake, causing bedlam at their grandmother's Knitting Circle meeting. Tongue-in-cheek text will have the reader laughing with each turn of the page while looking at the colorful, detailed drawings.

One day, while Florence and Eric are visiting Granny and Grandpa Mutton, they are sent to Miss Lavinia Bleating's house to fetch the cake she has made for Granny's Knitting Circle that afternoon. Meanwhile, Lavinia's sister, Muriel, comes home with her new, scrumptious-looking hat and leaves it in the front hall. The little lambs arrive and pick up the wrong box. When Muriel is ready to go out again, "there is just her hat to put on. And what an elegant hat it is. Why! Those cherries look almost real! She puts it firmly on her head. Aaargh!"

Back at the Muttons', "everyone is looking forward to a nice cup of tea and a slice of dear Lavinia's cake. It looks almost too good to eat. . . ." Children will delight in predicting the spirited mayhem that follows and concludes this hilarious story while the little lambs look on innocently, completely unaware of what they've done.

Program Description for
"Florence and Eric Take the Cake"
(Show #704)

LeVar looks into outrageous imitations of the real thing in "Florence and Eric Take the Cake." Kids suggest extraordinary cakes they would like to taste. And at Hansen's Bakery in Los Angeles, the most incredible cakes are made to order. Viewers watch as huge vats of batter are baked, sculpted, and frosted into a basketball, a towering cheeseburger, a perfectly pink pig, and even a racy blue sports car.

LeVar runs into Frankenstein, the Little Rascals, and Superman—statues one and all at the MovieLand Wax Museum. It's LeVar's turn to be immortalized in wax, and David Robert Cellitti does the honors. Using photos for reference, David sculpts LeVar's head in green clay. From there, he makes a mold, and then a hollow wax shell. LeVar selects eyes and teeth for his double and helps David place them. Once finished, the wax LeVar is ready for the *Reading Rainbow* exhibit. LeVar is beside himself—literally!

George Shrinks
Written and illustrated by William Joyce
HarperCollins

Here is a delightfully funny fantasy about a boy named George who wakes up one morning to find that he's the size of a mouse. Adorable illustrations and comical text combine to tell the adventures of George's *most* unusual day. Readers will get a kick out of adapting to becoming very small in this frolicking tale.

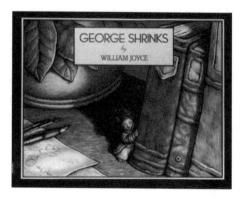

While his parents are out, George dreams that he is small. He wakes up to find that it's true! He also finds a note with instructions for the day: clean his room, get breakfast, and watch his "little" brother. George does precisely what his parents have asked (as well as any mouse-sized boy is able to do) and finds that once-mundane tasks such as doing the dishes or getting the mail can pose some interesting challenges when you're not full size. A run-in with the family cat bursts the fantasy, but the fun never ends in this comic adventure when George shrinks.

Please refer to the program description for "Imogene's Antlers." *George Shrinks* **is a Review Book in this episode.**

Gregory, the Terrible Eater

By Mitchell Sharmat

Illustrated by Jose Aruego and Ariane Dewey

Four Winds Press, a division of Macmillan Publishing Co.

Eating right takes on a whole new meaning when the family involved is made up of goats! With this upside-down, turned-around tale, boldly illustrated with cartoonlike characters, children will have a healthy laugh as they discover that junk food isn't nec-

essarily what they always thought it was. The irony of this story will appeal to even the pickiest of eaters and their parents.

Gregory is a terrible eater. His parents try to give him well-balanced meals of rugs, old shoes, boxes, and bottle caps, staples for *any* healthy growing goat, but Gregory refuses to eat, stating he would prefer some fruits, vegetables, eggs, and fish. His parents don't know what to do. They spend their evenings silently eating the newspaper as they ponder the problem.

Dr. Ram checks Gregory. "I've treated picky eaters before," he says. "They have to develop a taste for good food slowly. Try giving Gregory one new food each day until he eats everything." That night for dinner, Mother Goat gives Gregory spaghetti and a shoelace in tomato sauce. "Not too bad," says Gregory. In time, Gregory learns to like everything. His parents are pleased but notice that now Gregory won't *stop* eating. Items like Mother's sewing basket and Father's toolbox are missing. Gregory has eaten them!

To help the out-of-control Gregory, Mr. and Mrs. Goat go to the town dump and get lots of junk food—flat tires, a barber pole, half a car—and watch Gregory as he eats and eats and eats . . . until suddenly Gregory doesn't want any more and doesn't feel well. "I think Gregory ate too much junk," says Father Goat. Lesson learned, the next morning, Gregory requests a moderate breakfast of scrambled eggs, two pieces of waxed paper, and a glass of orange juice. The three sit down to enjoy a pleasant and sensible meal together.

Program Description for
"Gregory, the Terrible Eater"
(Show #111)

Food is the topic du jour in "Gregory, the Terrible Eater." A stop by the Barnyard Cafe serves up some laughs as LeVar finds himself in a restaurant run by goats! When they say "blue plate special," they mean it.

To see what's really on the menu for goats and other animals, LeVar visits the San Diego Zoo. Goats eat tree branches, otters prefer eggs, and tortoises think hibiscus blossoms a tasty treat. Scenes of feeding time at the zoo are accompanied by the bouncy Caribbean-flavored song "Everybody Likes to Eat." At the Hotel Intercontinental, four kids learn their way around the kitchen from one of New York's top chefs.

Imogene's Antlers

Written and illustrated by David Small
Crown Publishers

This story is guaranteed to tickle your funny bone every time. In it, Imogene, a normal, healthy girl, gets up one day to find herself bedecked with the most unusual protuberance, causing a riotous day for her exasperated family. David Small's elaborate illustrations enhance the sparest of text, making this nonsensical story a joy to read again and again.

"On Thursday, when Imogene woke up, she found she had grown antlers. Getting dressed was difficult, and going through a door now took some thinking." Determinedly, Imogene dresses and manages to get herself downstairs, where her mother promptly faints and the rest of the family simply stares. Everyone tries to remedy the situation (or live with it; the kitchen maid dries some towels on Imogene's antlers and Mrs. Perkins, the cook, announces, "You'll be lots of fun to decorate come Christmas!") The doctor, school principal, and even a milliner try but cannot help.

By the end of the day, Imogene finds herself exhausted and retires to her bedroom. The next morning, Imogene peeks into the kitchen, and her problem seems to be solved . . . until she enters the room and displays her fully-fanned peacock tail!

Program Description for
"Imogene's Antlers"
(Show #403)

LeVar visits the Philadelphia Zoo in "Imogene's Antlers." How an animal looks says a lot about how and where it lives. LeVar meets animals and their keepers to learn more about this—for example, flamingos are pink because of the shrimp they eat. A lighthearted music video looks at fashionable animal styles and how they all have their own interesting accessories.

Viewers go behind the scenes with the Quaker City String Band, better known as the Mummers. Using sequins, satin, chiffon, brocade, and more, the Mummers create outrageous sea creature costumes—including shrimp, lobster, and sardines. In full fish regalia, the Mummers march, play their instruments, and dance!

Meanwhile Back at the Ranch

By Trinka Hakes Noble
Illustrated by Tony Ross
Dial Books for Young Readers, a division of Penguin Books USA Inc.

This knee-slapper is a comical yet harmless farce on the traditional American farmer and his wife. When Rancher Hicks goes into town to find some excitement, ironically, it is his wife who sees all the action while she stays at home. Droll text and deadpan illustrations make this a funny tale which children will find a hoot.

Nothing much ever happens out at the ranch, so Rancher Hicks heads into town looking for some action. There, he finds twelve-year-old wanted posters and watches a turtle cross the road. Meanwhile, back at the ranch, it seems that this is his wife Elna's lucky day, from a prize-winning phone call and striking oil out in the potato field to an unexpected visit from the President! The ranch becomes as glitzy and gaudy as it was sparse and dull before. When her husband returns, Elna is sorry to hear she's missed all the excitement in town. Farmer Hicks looks beyond Elna toward their ranch and says, "What the hay . . .?!?!?!?!"

Program Description for
"Meanwhile Back at the Ranch"
(Show #414)

LeVar rides a stagecoach into Old Tucson, Arizona, a town where everything—and everyone—looks the way it did when the West was wild. He gets all "duded up" like a cowboy, and the song montage "Everybody Says Howdy to a Cowboy" accompanies LeVar across town.

Archival pictures spotlight cowboys and cowgirls, revealing details about the clothes they wore and the lives they led. Stunt horseback rider Wendy Wolverton demonstrates the tricks of her trade, including hanging sideways off the saddle and riding standing up, even with two horses! This western show ends with—what else?—LeVar riding off into the sunset.

Miss Nelson Is Back

By Harry Allard
Illustrated by James Marshall
Houghton Mifflin Co.

When the kids in Room 207 are unruly with their substitute teacher, their ill but insightful teacher finds she must teach them a lesson they will never forget. In their eminent style, Harry Allard and James Marshall have outdone themselves in this second work in a trilogy of Miss Nelson books. Children will be rolling in the halls as they predict the outcome of this roaringly funny story.

Miss Nelson must have her tonsils taken out and will be missing school for a week. At recess the older kids say that this means Miss Viola Swamp, the meanest substitute in the whole world, may show up. Fortunately, however, Mr. Blandsworth, the principal, fills in instead. Bored to tears by his corny card tricks and slides of his goldfish, the kids hatch a plot. Disguised as Miss Nelson, the kids relieve the principal, who returns to his office, leaving the youngsters to play hooky. "Heading back to school, they passed Miss Nelson's house. Miss Nelson couldn't believe her eyes. 'Those are my kids!' "

In their classroom that afternoon, "Miss Nelson's kids were spending an agreeable afternoon. They were very pleased with themselves. 'We should do this more often,' " they said. They did not notice the figure out in the hall. Viola Swamp! Under her iron rule, the kids straighten up immediately and feel great relief when she finally leaves the classroom. A minute later, Miss Nelson appears. She doesn't mention a word of what's happened, and the children wonder how she could have missed Miss Swamp out in the hall.

Program Description for
"Miss Nelson Is Back"
(Show #102)

The secret password is "surprise" in "Miss Nelson Is Back." It's his birthday, and LeVar is given clues that send him all over town. Along the way, he learns a thing or two about disguises and illusions. LeVar gets a makeover from Tom Burman and a team of makeup artists who create special makeup effects for the movies. With the help of facial prosthetics, spirit gum, and more, LeVar undergoes an amazing transformation.

Another birthday clue sends LeVar to a show with magician Harry Blackstone. LeVar gets in on the act, and Blackstone saws him in two! And seeing isn't always believing when LeVar twinkles the ivories on a player piano that plays even when he takes his hands off the keys. His treasure hunt comes to an end with a special birthday surprise—can you guess what it is?

Multicultural

Abiyoyo

A story-song by Pete Seeger
Illustrated by Michael Hays
Macmillan Publishing Co.

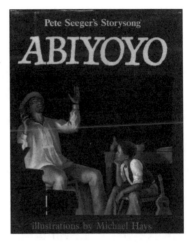

It's not until disaster strikes that a group of narrow-minded villagers learn the lesson that even annoying or eccentric people can play a valuable role in the community and deserve to be included. Pete Seeger has adapted an old South African folktale about a monster who eats people. When the monster is tricked into dancing, he dances himself into a fit, whereupon a magician dispatches him immediately. Michael Hays's illustrations in this adaptation are rich in color, graphic yet amusing and not frightening to a child's eye. In fact, Abiyoyo, giant that he is, looks very goofy.

When a magician and his ukelele-playing son are banished from town for playing too many tricks on the local townspeople, they settle in a small cabin on the outskirts of the village and pass the time telling stories about a giant called Abiyoyo. "They said he was as tall as a tree and could eat people up. Of course, nobody believed the story, but they told it anyway."

One day the boy and his father awaken to a giant shadow blocking the new day's sun. What's that? the boy wonders. It's Abiyoyo! "With long fingernails 'cause he never cut 'em . . . slobbery teeth 'cause he never brushed 'em, stinking feet 'cause he didn't wash 'em, and matted hair 'cause he didn't comb it." Just as Abiyoyo reaches for them with his huge claws, the boy begins singing and playing his ukelele. Now, this giant has never heard a song with his name in it before. "A-BI-YO-YO, A-BI-YO-YO." He smiles and begins to dance, faster and faster until he falls down flat on the ground. Quick as a wink, the father is able to—*zoop!*—dissipate the giant before their very eyes. Cheering and clapping, the townspeople are so impressed with the fellows' bravery, they once again welcome them to the town. All ends well. This is a wonderfully told story about good and evil. Read it, tell it, and sing it often, for children will be asking for it by name.

Program Description for
"Abiyoyo"
(Show #405)

In "Abiyoyo," LeVar hosts a show all about stories told with music. One of his in-studio guests is author/folk singer Pete Seeger, who narrates and sings a delightful adaptation of his book *Abiyoyo*. Pete tells how he came up with the tale because his children didn't want just a lullaby, they wanted a story too. The episode's book reviews are done with LeVar interviewing the three kid critics.

Run-D.M.C. rap and rhyme about themselves and books— "from the front to the back as pages turn, reading is a fun way to learn!" A visit with the Melody Stewart Dance Company shows how stories can be told with instrumental music and movement.

Amazing Grace

By Mary Hoffman
Illustrated by Caroline Binch
Dial Books for Young Readers, a division of Penguin Books USA Inc.

When a young girl is faced with discrimination by her classmates, she turns to her family for support and discovers that she can achieve anything she sets her mind to do. This kindergartner, named Grace, would like to play the lead in the school play, *Peter Pan,* but she is told by the other children that because she is black and a girl, she can't. The range of emotions Grace feels and her resulting triumph will be shared by the reader as the story unfolds with amazingly expressive watercolor illustrations.

Grace loves stories. Every time she hears one, she acts it out, always giving herself the most exciting part; Joan of Arc, Anansi the Spider, Hiawatha, or Mowgli, Grace is a natural and talented performer. So when her teacher announces that they will be putting on the play *Peter Pan*, Grace knows exactly who she wants to be. "You can't be Peter—that's a boy's name," says Raj. "You can't be Peter Pan," whispers Natalie. "He isn't black." But Grace keeps her hand up.

That night, despite her bravado, Grace is sad. She tells her mother and grandmother what happened. "Ma looked angry. But before she could speak, Nana said, '. . . You can be anything you want, Grace, if you put your mind to it.' " The next Saturday, Nana takes Grace to the ballet to see *Romeo and Juliet*. Grace notices that the beautiful young ballerina playing Juliet is African American. This gives Grace the confidence to believe in herself.

Auditions are held the following Monday. "When it was Grace's turn to be Peter, she knew exactly what to do and all the words to say—she had been Peter Pan all weekend. She took a deep breath and imagined herself flying." After the auditions, "there was no doubt who would be Peter Pan. *Everyone* voted for Grace. `You were fantastic!' whispered Natalie." The play and this book are a huge success. *Amazing Grace* will foster inward pride and boost the confidence of every reader.

Program Description for
"Amazing Grace"
(Show #906)

In "Amazing Grace," viewers meet three women who, like Grace, have broken barriers and succeeded when others told them they couldn't. Comedian and actor Whoopi Goldberg shares stories of her success and talks about early characters like "the girl with the luxurious blond hair."

Sheila Haynes works in the boiler room in a New York City Housing Project—not the first place people look for a woman. But Sheila gets the job done right. Lauren Turner plays high school hockey—and as viewers watch her on the ice in practice and a game, there's no doubt she's as good as the boys.

Galimoto

By Karen Lynn Williams
Illustrated by Catherine Stock
Lothrop, Lee & Shepard Books

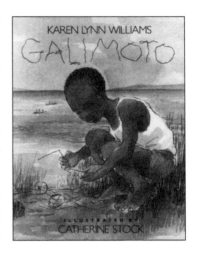

Set in Malawi, Africa, this is the story of an inventive young boy who is determined to make a galimoto despite his brother's teasing. Galimotos are push toys, traditionally made by children in this culture, out of old wires, sticks, cornstalks, or even pieces of yam to form cars, trucks, bicycles, trains, and helicopters. Vibrant watercolor paintings depict the small village where the boy lives. This is a creative, satisfying story.

Kondi has been saving bits of wire for something special. " 'I shall make a galimoto,' Kondi told his brother, Ufulu. Ufulu laughed. 'A boy with only seven years cannot make such a toy. You don't have enough wire.' 'I will get enough wire,' Kondi answered." Through the village he goes, collecting pieces of wire from his uncle, from behind the flour mill, in the trash heap, and from his friend Munde. "Then he began. The thick wires made the frame. He wrapped the very thinnest wires at the joints to hold the galimoto together. 'My galimoto will be a pickup,' Kondi planned." That night after working all afternoon, Kondi proudly leads his friends in a parade, all with their precious galimotos in tow.

Program Description for
"Galimoto"
(Show #709)

Wire, wire, wire—it makes the world and "Galimoto" go around. A montage kicks off this tribute to wire, spotlighting all kinds of everyday items that are made with this versatile material. LeVar tries his hand at pipe-cleaner art, with some impressive results. Artist Ele McKay uses wire to draw in space, creating two- and three-dimensional sculptures of animals, faces, and more. Calling hers an "ornery medium," Ele says she tames the wire, then twists and paints it as she sees fit.

Albuquerque's Sandia Peak Tramway is another example of wire at work—the cables that span the mountainsides are made from many wires the size Ele used, twisted tightly together. Some people really put their lives on the line—walking the tightrope in the Ringling Brothers Barnum & Bailey Circus. Viewers meet a family of acrobats who ride bikes, "leapfrog," and even lie down on the tightrope wire.

Jambo Means Hello: Swahili Alphabet Book

By Muriel Feelings
Illustrated by Tom Feelings
Dial Books for Young Readers, a division of Penguin Books USA Inc.

This book introduces the reader to the language of Swahili by listing twenty-four words, one word for every letter of the Swahili alphabet (there is no Q or X). On each page, we read the letter and the pronunciation, definition, and brief description of the accompanying word. The black-and-white drawings clearly illustrate traditional East African life; a map of Africa showing in which countries Swahili, the most commonly spoken language in Africa, is spoken, makes this an excellent vehicle for discussions of other cultures or for children of African ancestry to learn more of their own heritage.

With double-spread paintings, saying hello or seeing a tropical classroom scene becomes vivid in the reader's mind. After an interesting introduction, the book commences with "A, Arusi is a wedding. When two people marry, it is an important event for the village as well as for their families. It is celebrated with drumming, dancing, and much food for all." Many people, places, and objects later, the book concludes with "Z, Zeze is a stringed instrument. This musical instrument is the great-great-grandfather of the banjo and the guitar we know today. The xylophone, too, comes to us from Africa."

Please refer to the program description for "Mufaro's Beautiful Daughters." *Jambo Means Hello: Swahili Alphabet Book* is a Review Book in this episode.

Sweet Clara and the Freedom Quilt

Deborah Hopkinson
Illustrated by James Ransome
Alfred A. Knopf

A young black seamstress and slave overcomes her suppression in a most resourceful and courageous way; for intricately woven in her scrap quilt, she has stitched a map of the land, forming a freedom quilt—one that no master will suspect. The illustrations are outstanding, vivid, and inspirational. The quilt looks real enough to touch. Based on fact, this tale recounts a little-known chapter in African-American history that took place over one hundred years ago.

Determined to find her mother, from whom she was separated, and freedom for herself and other slaves, Clara, a seamstress in the Big House on Home Plantation, begins to piece together her freedom quilt. "When I was off work, I went to visit people in the Quarters—I started askin' what fields was what. Then I started piecin' the scraps of cloth with the scraps of things I was learnin'. Aunt Rachel say, `Sweet Clara, what kind of pattern you makin' in that quilt? Aine no pattern I ever seen.' 'I don't know, Aunt Rachel. I'm just patchin it together as I go.' She looked at me long, but she just nodded."

Over time, the quilt gets bigger and bigger, "and if folk knew what I was doin', no one said. But they came by the sewin room to pass the time of day whenever they could." Finally, the quilt is finished. Clara and another slave, Jack, flee the plantation and leave the quilt behind for others to use. They follow the course of her quilt that is imprinted in her mind: "Now I could see the real things. There was the old tree struck down by lightning, the winding road near the creek, the hunting path through the swamp. It was like being in a dream you already dreamed."

Clara and Jack find her mother and survive the trek to Canada. As time goes by, other survivors tell her that her quilt showed *them* the way too. Clara is pleased to help but says "Sometimes I wish I could sew a quilt that would spread over the whole land, and the people just follow the stitches to freedom, as easy as taking a Sunday walk." This is an important, deeply moving story, empowered by emotion, that commands the reader's attention in the gentlest of ways.

Please refer to the program description for "Follow the Drinking Gourd." *Sweet Clara and the Freedom Quilt* **is a Review Book in this episode.**

Tar Beach

Written and illustrated by Faith Ringgold
Crown Publishers

Poverty, prejudice, and unhappiness all but disappear when a little girl dreams she can fly. She soars so high, nothing oppressive can reach her. This book is set in 1939, and magically weaves together fiction, autobiography, and African-American history that will inspire a whole new appreciation for the word "freedom." Readers will find that wishes do come true in this story, which was inspired by a quilt made by the

author. Although there are new paintings, the text, the borders, and the cover art are from Ringgold's story quilt. This book is presented in a unique medium and carries a strong message for all to hear.

While her family is up on "tar beach," the rooftop of their Harlem apartment building, having a picnic dinner, as they often do, Cassie experiences a dream come true. Over the George Washington Bridge she soars, exclaiming, "I can fly—yes, fly. Me, Cassie Louise Lightfoot, only eight years old and in the third grade, and I can fly. That means I am free to go wherever I want for the rest of my life." She claims the city as her own—from the ice cream factory to the members-only Union Building that will not allow Daddy to join because his daddy wasn't a member. Later she takes her brother, Be Be, with her, explaining that "it's very easy, anyone can fly. All you need is somewhere to go that you can't get to any other way. The next thing you know, you're flying among the stars." Join Cassie and Be Be in this magical story where the sky's the limit.

Program Description for
"Tar Beach"
(Show #806)

LeVar spends a day up on the roof in "Tar Beach." This urban oasis in the sky is a great escape on a summer's day. From his tar beach, LeVar has a beautiful view of the George Washington Bridge, just like Cassie. Viewers go to the very top of this bridge to see how the lights on the "necklace" are changed, and down to the anchorage for a look at what holds this giant steel structure together.

Viewers tour New York City's rooftops and meet a man who raises pigeons and a woman with a gorgeous garden. The classic Drifters tune "Up on the Roof" is brought to life in a wonderful music video.

Thirteen Moons on Turtle's Back

By Joseph Bruchac and Jonathan London
Illustrated by Thomas Locker
Philomel

This is a collection of poems, based on Native American legends, explaining the thirteen moons of the year. Appropriate titles are followed by extraordinary poems, bringing out the wonders of each month in our calendar year. The combined talents of Abenaki storyteller Joseph Bruchac and poet Jonathan London are breathtaking. Spectacular oil paintings by Thomas Locker honor these legends and our natural world. Although some Native American nations use several names for one moon, in this book, one moon story from each of thirteen different nations has been selected, in an effort to represent the different Native American regions of the continent.

"Many Native American people look at turtle's back as a sort of calendar, with its pattern of thirteen large scales standing for the thirteen moons in each year. . . . It reminds us that all things are connected and we must try to live in balance." From the Anishinabes' Maple Sugar Moon to the Senecas' Strawberry Moon to the Pomos' Moon When Acorns Appear, the Native American legend explains the great power of the natural world. Listen to these poems and respect them, for they hold the secrets to the mysteries of the Earth.

Please refer to the program description for "And Still the Turtle Watched." *Thirteen Moons on Turtle's Back* **is a Review Book in this episode.**

Uncle Nacho's Hat

A bilingual Spanish/English book
Adapted by Harriet Rohmer
Illustrated by Veg Reisberg
Children's Book Press, San Francisco

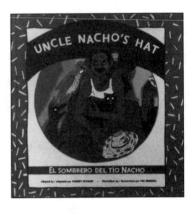

This bilingual folktale from Nicaragua is about a man who must make some changes in his life, but doesn't know how until his young niece shows him the way. The text is printed first in English and then in Spanish on each page, and the acrylic art is bordered by colorful designs. The author adapted this story from a performance by the Puppet Workshop of Nicaragua National Television, which uses the medium of folktales to inspire people to think critically about the way they conduct their lives.

Uncle Nacho is tired of his old hat. It is full of holes and does not keep the sun out of his eyes. When his niece, Ambrosia, gives him a brand-new hat, he is very pleased but cannot seem to part with his old hat. Two times he finally throws it away only to find it returned to him by neighbors. When Ambrosia sees that her uncle is having a difficult time with this change, she says, "Stop worrying about the old hat, Uncle Nacho. Think about your new hat instead." Uncle Nacho sees what she means and promptly goes for a walk through town wearing his new hat, so that everyone, himself included, may get acquainted with the new Uncle Nacho.

Please refer to the program description for "Florence and Eric Take the Cake." *Uncle Nacho's Hat* is a Review Book in this episode.

Yagua Days

By Cruz Martel
Illustrated by Jerry Pinkney
Dial Books for Young Readers, a division of Penguin Books USA Inc.

A visit to Puerto Rico proves to be a cultural eye-opener for the boy in this story, especially when he finds out the meaning of a Yagua Day during their first day of rain. Many words in the text of this story are in Spanish, and the author provides a word list, including definitions and pronunciations. Join New Yorker Adan Riera as he takes a trip with his parents to the motherland to visit never-before-seen relatives and find delight in the rich heritage he finds there.

Visiting the family is fun for everyone. Until now, Adan had no idea how large his extended family really is. A trip through groves of Grandfather's fruit trees brings them baskets full of oranges, *mangos*, *mapenes* (breadfruit), *ñames* (similar to a potato), and coconuts. Adan has only seen these fruits delivered by truck to his family's store in New York City. These are amazing! That night, Uncle's sore knee indicates that tomorrow it will rain. This is good news in Puerto Rico.

The next morning, Adan wakes to find his whole family wearing bathing suits and ready to go. It's raining! Quickly, Adan joins them, and in the forest he hears shouts and swishing noises. His father hands him a huge discarded frond from a palm tree. " 'And this is what we do with it,' said his father. He ran, then belly-flopped on the yagua. He skimmed down the grass, sailed up into the air, and vanished over the ledge. His mother found another yagua and did the same." Soon, Adan joins them, and others, sliding down the butter-slick grass, soaking wet, and zipping into the river pool at the bottom. The day is spent sliding and climbing back up, over and over again. What fun! Adan can now appreciate a rainy day, a Yagua Day! This has been a trip he'll never forget. If you can't make it to Puerto Rico on your own, join Adan in this extraordinary adventure.

Program Description for
"My Little Island"
(Show #415)

(*Yagua Days* is a Review Book in this episode.)

Memories of the Caribbean island of Montserrat fill the book adaptation of "My Little Island." LeVar travels to this tropical paradise and visits the people and places that inspired the book.

The town market bustles with activity and gives LeVar a taste of island life. Exotic fruits line the tables—papaya, pineapple, and watermelon that's half the size and missing its trademark stripes. At night, LeVar searches for "mountain chicken." That's the local nickname for frogs! By lantern light, they find not only frogs but an iguana too. As his vacation draws to a close, a steel drum band serenades LeVar with a calypso version of the *Reading Rainbow* theme.

Music

Barn Dance!

By Bill Martin Jr. and John Archambault
Illustrated by Ted Rand
Henry Holt and Co., Inc.

This is a delightful dream come true that captures the spirit of a full-moon night and the cadence of square dancing in infectious rhyming verse. Spend this magical night with a boy who hears unusual noises coming from the barn and finds himself drawn there to join the farm animals in a midnight, all-out, foot-stomping barn dance. Alive and alluring paintings will draw the reader from bed to the moonlit barn for a night of fun never to be forgotten. That the authors and artist request this book be read aloud will come as no surprise.

One night, in his old farmhouse, a boy is unable to sleep for the plunking of a fiddle that lures him out of bed. Stealing to the barn, he finds a scarecrow playing music with a crow on his shoulder, who calls, "Begin! Grab your partner an' jump right in!" At this, all the farm animals line up to follow the calls and "out came the skinny kid, a-tickin' an' a-tockin' an' a-hummin' an' a-yeein' an' a-rockin' an' a-sockin'. An' he danced his little toe through a hole in his stockin'!" Around and around and around they go until "the sky was warmin' up for the comin' of the day when the skinny kid . . . heard . . . the night owl . . . say, mornin's comin' closer . . . mornin's comin' closer . . . the magic time is over . . . night'll soon be gone . . ." Running across the field and tiptoeing through the house, the boy jumps back into bed, "with the wonders of the barn dance . . . dancin' in his head."

Program Description for
"Barn Dance!"
(Show #506)

LeVar's in Tennessee for a down-home show about country culture in "Barn Dance." It's more fun than a jar full of fireflies! A little bluegrass music sets the stage for a visit to a man who's been making fiddles most of his life. Viewers watch as he carefully carves the wood and works it into a fiddle. Each is unique, he says; they don't all sound exactly the same.

Down at the barn, folks are practicing their "clogging." It's like a combination of tap dance and square dancing. Colorful steps are called out, guiding everyone through "birdie in a cage," "dive for an oyster, dive for a pearl," and "old crow flap your wings." Everyone kicks up their heels for the show's finale as the barn dance begins.

Berlioz the Bear

Written and illustrated by Jan Brett

G. P. Putnam's Sons, a division of Putnam & Grosset Book Group

This is an amusing, cumulative tale in which a band of bear musicians are due to play for a town ball when their bandwagon gets stuck in a hole in the road. A strange buzzing in the band leader's double bass turns out to be a surprise that saves the day. Intricate border art reveals the Bavarian village animals arriving at the square, setting up, and patiently waiting for the music to begin. These and the larger detailed illustrations are some  of Jan Brett's finest work. Readers will linger over each painting right through to the climactic ending.

"*Zum, zum, buzz . . . zum, zum, buzz . . .*" What could that strange sound coming from Berlioz the Bear's double bass be? Distracted by the buzzing, Berlioz doesn't watch where the cart carrying his all-bear orchestra goes, the wagon gets stuck in a hole, and the mule *will not* pull it out. Along comes a rooster, a cat, a schnauzer, a billy goat, and even an ox, all of whom fail to free the bandwagon.

Berlioz instructs his band members to dress in their tailcoats and tune up so that they'll be ready to start as soon as they arrive. When the bow is pulled across the strings of his double bass, Berlioz is dismayed to hear "*zum . . . zum . . . buzz . . . buzzzz.*" All eyes land on Berlioz, when "out of the bass shot a very angry bee.

It had been disturbed once too often. The first thing it saw as it flew out of the bass was the hindquarters of the mule. *Buzzzzz.*" Before they know it, the mule jumps to his feet and pulls the bandwagon of musicians out of the hole and into the village, arriving at exactly eight o'clock! The audience is very impressed by such an entrance. Musicians and dancers alike have a wonderful evening, and, appropriately, Berlioz selects "Flight of the Bumble Bee" as an encore.

Program Description for
"Berlioz the Bear"
(Show #905)

Letting music be his guide, LeVar explores the city of New York in "Berlioz the Bear." He finds street musicians, who bring their show straight to an audience on the go. All over town, from the subway to the Battery, people are making music. There's a steel drum band on the Staten Island Ferry, a trio of violins in Central Park, the Women of the Calabash playing African music in midtown, and so much more.

Uptown, the Boys Choir of Harlem makes a most glorious sound under the direction of Dr. Walter Turnbull. Singing in the choir doesn't just give the boys musical inspiration. One says he's learned to be a leader; another feels more like a man now; and a third admits if he weren't in the choir, he would "probably be doing something stupid right now." Just like any sports team, the boys work together; they have even written a song of their own, called "The Joy of Singing."

Georgia Music

By Helen V. Griffith
Illustrated by James Stevenson
Greenwillow Books

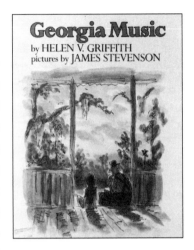

The love and understanding a grand-father shares with his granddaughter proves to be just the right medicine when he is forced to leave his home and loses his independence. Gentle words are enhanced by James Stevenson's emotional watercolor illustrations, making this a subtle story carrying a loud and clear message: Sometimes it's the youngest generation in the family that can be the most understanding.

A little girl takes a train from Baltimore to Georgia to visit her grandfather for the summer. "The old man never said how he felt about that, but he didn't seem to mind. The girl didn't mind either. She liked it right away." Together they tend the garden each morning and rest under a tree each afternoon to the sounds of the leaves, the crickets, and the bees. By evening the two sit on the porch, the old man playing his mouth organ in harmony with nature's sounds. "The old man said he was really playing for the crickets and the grasshoppers because they made music for him in the daytime. He said they liked it, and the girl thought so, too."

A time comes when the grandfather must leave his cabin and live with his family in Baltimore. It is the little girl who brings him the Georgia music he has missed so sorely when she picks up the mouth organ and begins to play. "Except it wasn't exactly music and they weren't real songs. They were the sounds she remembered from that Georgia summer—cricket chirps and tree frog trills and bee buzzes and bird twitters . . . and for a while it was like being right back in Georgia."

Please refer to the program description for "Berlioz the Bear." *Georgia Music* **is a Review Book in this episode.**

I Like the Music

By Leah Komaiko
Illustrated by Barbara Westman
HarperCollins

A young city girl with a passion for street music is introduced to an outdoor symphony in the park by her grandmother, with startling results. Barbara Westman's scintillating and detailed illustrations capture the flavor of a big city, and Leah Komaiko's savvy and rhythmic text makes this book an upbeat experience for any child. Be sure to read this poem out loud.

"I do not like this concert hall. This concert hall's no fun at all. The orchestra just plays and plays, I could be here for thirty days. And I must sit here in this seat, don't clap my hands, don't tap my feet. And Grandma says this is a treat." But this girl would much rather be outside with the street musicians: "I like the beat of my feet when my shoes hit the streets and I rapa-tapa-tapa on the hot concrete."

When Grandma suggests the symphony, her granddaughter is apprehensive, at best, until she hears more about it. "The dark? The park? Why Grandma, this treat sounds just right. I like the music late at night. . . ." And so they go to the park, where, just as the girl is feeling the anticipation, "it is all about to start. I can feel the flutes are fluttering all around my beating heart. . . ." She is given an added special treat because the conductor asks for a volunteer's help onstage.

Please refer to the program description for "Barn Dance!" *I Like the Music* **is a Review Book in this episode.**

Mama Don't Allow

Written and illustrated by Thacher Hurd
HarperCollins

This is a funny, jazzy tale inspired by the traditional American song "Mama Don't Allow," which will appeal to every noise-loving child around. Thacher Hurd's text is hilarious, with subtle text asides that are not to be missed. His art is bright, colorful, and childlike. Words and tune to this infectious song are provided.

Miles, the possum, receives a saxophone for his birthday. His incessant practicing drives him out of the house and into town, "where he met a drummer named Al; up Swamp Lane where he met a guitarist named Bert; and over Bayou Bridge where he met a trumpet player named Doc." They form a band—Miles and the Swamp Band—and have the time of their lives until they are driven out of town and down to the swamp by the quiet-preferring townspeople.

Some sharp-toothed, long-tailed alligators eye the delectable band and demurely suggest that they play at the Alligator Ball that Saturday night. The band agrees, and on that night, after a rollicking round of "Mama Don't Allow," they discover that the late-night menu features SWAMP BAND SOUP! The band changes its tune and succeeds in lulling the alligators to sleep—allowing the band to safely tiptoe away. Join Miles and his all-night, all-star band. Your toes will be tapping with each turn of the page.

Program Description for
"Mama Don't Allow"
(Show #310)

LeVar heads south to get a glimpse of swamp life in "Mama Don't Allow." He meets a naturalist from the New Orleans Zoo who introduces him to real live alligators. An alligator's jaws are the strongest part of its body. It has sixty teeth, and when one falls out, it can grow another . . . that's three thousand teeth in one lifetime.

Viewers go behind the scenes at the adaptation of the book *Mama Don't Allow* and meet Fred Newman, who uses only his voice and imagination to make all the characters and musical instruments in the book come to life. Aboard the riverboat *Creole Queen*, LeVar meets jazz musicians who improvise a song, showing how they speak to each other through their instruments.

Miranda
Written and illustrated by Tricia Tusa
Macmillan Publishing Co.

In this book a family learns to abandon drastic measures and practice the art of compromise to regain harmony in its household. Miranda, a young classical pianist, discovers boogie-woogie music. When she is forbidden to practice it, she quits playing the piano altogether until the silence becomes so deafening that she and her family decide that Miranda may play many kinds of music, including boogie-woogie. Tricia Tusa's expressive and comical drawings amplify the family's exaggerated opinions representing how reluctant to change we sometimes are.

Miranda loves to play the piano. Whether it's classical for her family, the school anthem for the kids in her class, or scales for her piano teacher, it doesn't matter—she loves it all. Then one day Miranda is walking home from school and hears a one-man band playing boogie-woogie. Miranda runs home to practice her newfound passion. "Playing boogie-woogie makes Miranda very happy. Miranda's playing boogie-woogie makes everyone else very, very unhappy." Their nagging comments drive Miranda to quit playing the piano altogether. Everyone finds they are miserable with the silence and her mom finally says okay, she can play boogie-woogie. "Why can't I play both—classical and boogie-woogie?" Miranda replies. And once again there is music!

Please refer to the program description for "Mama Don't Allow."
Miranda **is a Review Book in this episode.**

Ty's One-Man Band

By Mildred Pitts Walter
Illustrated by Margot Tomes
Four Winds Press, a division of Macmillan Publishing Co.

With a little ingenuity and the help of a talented new friend, a child learns that sometimes the simplest things in life bring the most joy. A gifted and unusual stranger visits a young boy's town and, using everyday items for musical instruments, magically transforms the cantankerous townspeople on a hot, humdrum summer evening into a lively, music-loving, and unified group. Imaginatively told, this enriching story celebrates simplicity.

Another blisteringly hot day in Ty's town. To cool off, he goes to the pond, where he observes, unnoticed, a peg-legged man named Andro who can juggle and make music with just a cup and a spoon. When they meet later, Andro promises to perform in the town square at sundown. Perform he does, drawing in the whole town to share the sparse instruments—a washboard, comb, spoons, and a pail—as they begin clapping and tapping their toes to the music of Ty's one-man band.

"Boys and girls, mothers and fathers, even the babies clapped their hands. Some danced on the street." Only Ty sees his friend slip away into the night, and he is thankful that Andro has offered so much to so many people.

Program Description for
"Ty's One-Man Band"
(Show #115)

Music and sounds, the rhythms of life, are the themes of "Ty's One-Man Band." On a walk in the park, LeVar finds a real live one-man band—with fifty-five instruments! A performance music video features actor Ben Vereen dancing around a playground and singing about everyday sounds that sound like music. LeVar meets an a cappella group, who show how they use their voices as their musical instruments.

Reading Rainbow musical director Steve Horelick shares with viewers his tricks of the trade. With the help of computers, Steve is a modern one-man band who has scores of sounds available by touching a key or twisting a knob. An animated song about onomatopoeia shows how some words sound like what they are.

Physically Challenged

The Handmade Alphabet

Written and illustrated by Laura Rankin
Dial Books for Young Readers, a division of
Penguin Books USA Inc.

A celebration of communication, *The Handmade Alphabet* invites children to practice and master the visual language of American Sign Language. The manual alphabet, an integral part of ASL, is made up of twenty-six different hand positions representing the twenty-six written letters of the alphabet. This ABC book is an elegant, creative tribute to the visual language. On each page the hand signs a letter and is linked with a word that begins with a corresponding letter of the written alphabet. The hands are multicultural and multigenerational, a reminder that anyone can learn the manual alphabet.

Children will recognize the letters on each page not only by the letter printed, but also from the clever images intertwined with each hand. *B* has transparent bubbles floating all around. *M* reflects the back of the hand in a mirror while the hand faces forward, unobstructed. X is a skeletal X-ray of the hand while in the X position. Just in case, there is an index at the end of the book.

Please refer to the program description for "Silent Lotus." *The Handmade Alphabet* **is a Review Book in this episode.**

Silent Lotus

Written and illustrated by Jeanne M. Lee
Farrar, Straus & Giroux

Great accomplishments are not always loudly announced. In this story a deaf and mute Cambodian girl proves herself capable beyond anyone's dreams when her parents acquaint her with the fine art of temple dancing. The author saw the decorations of the twelfth-century temple at Angkor Wat and was inspired to write this story. Set in the Kampuchea of long ago, this book eloquently brings to life the thousand-year-old tradition of the Cambodian court ballet, and the part a talented heroine plays in it.

A beautiful daughter is born to a couple who live on the edge of the lake. Lotus is unable to hear or speak, and so they communicate with gestures. Lotus has no friends, and her happiest times are when "she walked among the herons, cranes, and white egrets, joining them in their graceful steps." To assuage her unhappiness, her parents take her to the temple in the city where a group of graceful women are dancing to the beat of drums and cymbals. Lotus feels the vibrations and imitates their steps perfectly. The king sees her and invites her to learn to dance the tales of the gods and kings.

"As time passed, silent Lotus began to speak with her hands, body and feet. She loved to dance the tales of the gods and kings. And, as she grew, the movements became as natural for her as the dances of the birds. Lotus made many friends. She was no longer lonely and sad. . . . It is said that Lotus became the most famous dancer in the Khmer kingdom."

Program Description for
"Silent Lotus"
(Show #910)

There are many ways to express yourself without using your voice—as LeVar finds out in "Silent Lotus." A mime shows how he communicates without speaking, and kids demonstrate other things you can say without saying a word.

A deaf woman named Terrylene teaches LeVar how to speak American Sign Language. She also talks about what it's like to be deaf, and points out that speaking is a skill, so people shouldn't judge a person's intelligence by their voice. Viewers meet eleven-year-old Bryan Chattoo, who shows that deaf people can do anything hearing people can . . . including dance.

Through Grandpa's Eyes
By Patricia MacLachlan
Illustrated by Deborah Ray
HarperCollins

A young boy learns that there are more ways of seeing than just with his eyes when he visits his grandfather, who is blind. Sensitively told, this story captures a child's and his grandparents' love for one another. It is a fine example of how, given the opportunity, your senses can become more acute than you ever thought possible.

It is always a special treat when John comes to visit his grandparents. His grandpa is blind and "has his own way of seeing." Through Grandpa's eyes, John learns to see in more ways than his own eyes allow. Sounds and smells tell him Grandma is downstairs cooking eggs and toast for breakfast. Playing the cello with Grandpa requires a delicate touch to get the notes just right. Grandpa is a capable person and an excellent role model. This is a beautiful book in which John discovers things that he could not otherwise know when he looks through Grandpa's "eyes."

Please refer to the program description for "Arthur's Eyes." *Through Grandpa's Eyes* **is a Review Book in this episode.**

Poetry and Verse

The Adventures of Taxi Dog

By Debra and Sal Barracca
Illustrated by Mark Buehner
Dial Books for Young Readers, a division of Penguin Books USA Inc.

When a stray dog is befriended by a New York City taxicab driver, his life changes over-night from one of loneliness to days filled with happy adventures. Joyous paintings with glorious colors depict the two insepara-ble friends and are accompa-nied by clever, rhyming verse.  The authors, dedicated to homeless animals everywhere, are donating a portion of the proceeds of this book to the Fund for Animals in New York City. This is a happy story that will warm the hearts of readers young and old.

Join Maxi and his newfound friend and owner, Jim, as they ride around town, picking up fares. The people they meet are always interesting, and Maxi makes sure that the passengers enjoy their ride. "We get such big tips on most of our trips—Jim is sur-prised at this treat. But he doesn't know that I put on a show for the passengers in the back seat!" Pictured here, a smiling Maxi is facing the backseat passengers and sporting a Groucho Marx nose, mustache, and glasses! "It's just like a dream, me and Jim—we're a team! I'm always there at his side. We never stand still, every day's a new thrill—come join us next time for a ride!"

Program Description for
"The Adventures of Taxi Dog"
(Show #707)

LeVar takes a spin as one of New York's finest—a cabdriver—in "The Adventures of Taxi Dog." He explains the ins and outs of cabbing it, and a hilarious montage spotlights all the ways people try to get a driver's attention when they hail a taxi.

As in the book, dogs make great friends. Viewers meet high school student Lisa Ferrerio and her canine companion, Kosmo. Because she has spina bifida, a degenerative bone disease, Lisa uses a wheelchair to get around. But Kosmo is always there for her, helping out at school, in the mall, and at home.

All the Colors of the Race

By Arnold Adoff
Illustrated by John Steptoe
Lothrop, Lee & Shepard Books

This is a powerful collection of thirty-seven beautiful poems written from the point of view of a child who has a Caucasian father and an African-American mother. Each poem celebrates human beings and is a reminder that "we are together" on this earth. The color of our skin and our racial differences give us special meaning; we should not allow these factors to interfere with how we feel about others. Arnold Adoff's words read like music, and John Steptoe's art, which portrays confident, loving family members, complements each poem.

I Am
Mama is black and Daddy is white
and I am black and I am white:
besides my age and sex and clarinet.

I Think the Real Color Is Behind the Color
I think the real color is behind the color
That skin on my face is for the cold mornings,
And the cold breezes of some summer afternoons.
Under that skin and under that face is the real race.

Please refer to program description for "Arthur's Eyes." *All the Colors of the Race* **is a Highlight Book in this episode.**

Bringing the Rain to Kapiti Plain

By Verna Aardema
Illustrated by Beatriz Vidal
The Dial Press, a division of Penguin Books USA Inc.

Reminiscent of "The House That Jack Built," this Nandi tale from Kenya tells the story of a young boy, Ki-pat, bringing the rain to the drought-plagued Kapiti Plain in cumulative refrain. The rhythm of the words makes this a perfect read-aloud. Vidal's folk-art illustrations are vivid and richly colorful.

"This was the shot that pierced the cloud and loosened the rain with thunder LOUD! A shot from the bow, so long and strong, and strung with a string, a leather thong; a bow for the arrow Ki-pat put together, with a slender stick and an eagle feather; from the eagle who happened to drop a feather, a feather that helped to change the weather . . . To green-up the grass, all brown and dead, that needed the rain from the cloud overhead—the big, black cloud, all heavy with rain, that shadowed the ground on Kapiti Plain."

Program Description for
"Bringing the Rain to Kapiti Plain"
(Show #104)

There's a 100 percent chance of a show about weather in "Bringing the Rain to Kapiti Plain." From the fanciful to the scientific, kids speculate about what thunder is. People indulge in a favorite rainy-day activity in a music video called "Puddle Hopping." LeVar shows how to make your very own rainbow simply by placing a half-full glass of water on a windowsill.

At the National Center for Atmospheric Research in Colorado, viewers meet scientists studying severe weather. Go behind the scenes to see how the radar works, and up in a plane that flies through thunderstorms. A lighthearted look at forecasting includes some people who watch caterpillars, squirrels, and bunions for clues about the coming weather.

Chipmunk Song

By Joanne Ryder
Illustrated by Lynne Cherry
Lodestar Books, an affiliate of Dutton Children's Books, a division of Penguin
Books USA Inc.

With imaginative perception, award-winning writer Joanne Ryder has written a poem about the change of seasons as seen through the eyes of a chipmunk. "Imagine you are someone small sleeping on a bed of leaves in a cool, dark room underground. Wake up,  small one. You cannot see the sun, but you feel the morning stir inside you." Lynne Cherry's lush paintings depict a small girl doing all that a chipmunk does to prepare for the coming winter. Enter the world of the forest, above ground and below, and savor the feeling with the turn of each incredible page.

Imagine you are a chipmunk. You are running—dashing from here to there—looking for acorns and watching for danger. Grasp the nuts and berries with your furry paws. "Chip chip chip chip chip. You sing a song. Other small ones hear it too and begin to sing. Chip chip chip chip and you know you are not alone." You are brown, soft, and furry. Stripes mark your furry face, your body, and your long tail. "All day long you run in the woods, filling your cheeks with acorns to hide in your home underground." Then one day, when the air is cold, you stay inside of your dark tunnel. The doorway is filled with dirt, and you sleep . . . until next spring when the cycle begins again. Large or small, let your imagination run free with this make-believe yet remarkably accurate poem.

Please refer to the program description for "The Salamander Room." *Chipmunk Song* **is a Review Book in this episode.**

Daydreamers

By Eloise Greenfield
Illustrated by Tom Feelings
Dial Books for Young Readers, a division of Penguin Books USA Inc.

Pen-and-ink as well as pencil sketches adorn this book which astutely shares the sentiments of girls and boys growing up African-American. Tom Feelings has sensitively drawn each portrait with a loving hand. Eloise Greenfield, inspired by the drawings, has created an evocative poem that brings the portraits to life. This quiet poem can be savored by readers of all ages.

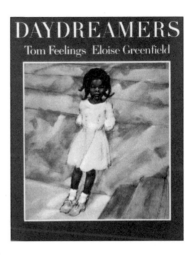

This work captures those brief moments between thought and action that fill every child's day. The various children drawn look off distantly or directly at the reader, offering a moment of thoughtful silence. All aged children are included, because all ages daydream. "Dreamers. Thinking up new ways, looking toward new days, planning new tries, asking new whys. Before long, hands will start to move again. Eyes turn outward, bodies shift for action but for this moment they are still. . . ."

Program Description for
"Bea and Mr. Jones"
(Show #103)

(*Daydreamers* is a Highlight Book in this episode.)

In the book adaptation in "Bea and Mr. Jones," a little girl and her father switch places—he goes to kindergarten and she goes to the office! LeVar decides he needs a vacation too. Digging into the costume rack, he suits up as a police officer, king, Dracula, and more. LeVar says he likes being an actor because he gets to see how other people live. Kids talk about who they would be if they could be anyone in the world.

Poems from the highlight book *Daydreamers* are brought to life with dramatic interpretations. Viewers meet twelve-year-old Jason Hardman, who made his dream come true—he started the town library in Elsinore, Utah, with ten thousand books.

Fathers, Mothers, Sisters, and Brothers: A Collection of Family Poems

By Mary Ann Hoberman
Illustrated by Marylin Hafner
Joy Street Books/Little, Brown and Co.

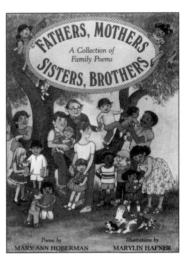

This fine collection of poems cele-brates virtually every kind of family possible. From large family to small; adoptive mother, single father, half brother, and stepsister—we're all included in this witty and thoughtful book. Each poem is expressed from a child's point of view, with multicul-tural art to illustrate the love, warmth, anger, and frustration we feel about family life, no matter where we are in the pecking order.

"What is a family? Who is a family? Either a lot or a few is a fam-ily, but whether there's ten or there's two in *your* family, all of your family plus *you* is a family." So begins this series of poems, which moves on to the wonders of family life, in such poems as "Four Generations," "New Jacket," and "Eat It—It's Good for You!"

Universally inclusive, the final poem is called "Our Family Comes From 'Round the World." One of its verses reads: "We laugh and cry. We work and play. We help each other every day. The world's a lovely place to be because we are a family. Hurray, hurrah, hurrah, hurree. We're one big happy family!"

Please refer to the program description for "Through Moon and Stars and Night Skies." *Fathers, Mothers, Sisters, Brothers: A Collection of Family Poems* **is a Review Book in this episode.**

Honey, I Love and Other Love Poems

By Eloise Greenfield
Illustrated by Diane and Leo Dillon
HarperCollins

Here is a collection of sixteen heart-felt love poems written from an African-American child's perspective. Titles include "Fun," "I Look Pretty," "Harriet Tubman," and "Rope Rhyme." Each poem is decorated with portrait drawings as well as panoramic painted wood-blocks. The children in the illustrations capture the emotions that the words speak. This is a warm and fulfilling compilation.

By Myself

When I'm by myself
And I close my eyes
I'm a twin
I'm a dimple in a chin
I'm a room full of toys
I'm a squeaky noise
I'm a gospel song
I'm a gong
I'm a leaf turning red
I'm a loaf of brown bread
I'm a whatever I want to be
An anything I care to be

And when I open my eyes
What I care to be
Is me

Please refer to the program description for "Feelings." *Honey, I Love and Other Love Poems* is a Review Book in this episode.

Owl Moon

By Jane Yolen
Illustrated by John Schoenherr
Philomel Books

Crisply written in poetic style with riveting watercolor illustrations, this beautiful story is about hope and quiet rewards. Late one winter night, a little girl and her father trek into the snowy woods to go owling. It is very dark and very quiet in the woods. The girl has been looking forward to this honor for a long, long time and knows she must be very quiet. "Pa held up his hands. I stopped right where I was and waited. He looked up, as if searching the stars, as if reading a map up there. The moon made his face into a silver mask. Then he called: *whoo-whoo-who-who-who-whooooooo*, the sound of a Great Horned Owl." Then silence.

Again he calls out. And then again until suddenly an echo makes its way through the trees. "All of a sudden an owl shadow, part of the big tree shadow lifted off and flew right over us. We watched silently with heat in our mouths, the heat of all those words we had not spoken. The shadow hooted again." The anticipation and excitement the girl feels culminates in one illustration showing the magnificent and elusive Great Horned Owl staring at the two. The girl's hopes have come true. Savor this book in which human compatibility is shared with the natural world.

Program Description for
"Knots on the Counting Rope"
(Show #508)

(*Owl Moon* is a Review Book in this episode.)

The book adaptation in "Knots on a Counting Rope" is about a blind boy who gains courage each time his grandfather tells the story of how the child got his name, Boy Strength of Blue Horses. LeVar faces a challenge of his own—camping in the woods for a whole night all by himself. Kids talk about the last time they had to be really brave.

Anchorwoman Bree Walker shares her own inspirational story. Despite a physical disorder that made her hands and feet deformed, she decided to try to make it in TV—and at first people told her they didn't think viewers would watch her. But Bree persevered, eventually getting one of the best jobs in TV news— anchorwoman in New York City. Bree credits teachers and adults who encouraged her, and says that anyone who tells you "You can't," just doesn't know.

Snowy Day: Stories and Poems

Edited by Caroline Feller Bauer
Illustrated by Margot Tomes
HarperCollins

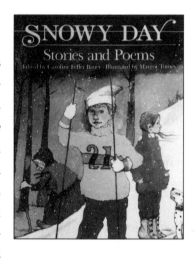

Snow is the common theme in this anthology of multicultural snowy-day poems, stories, facts, activities, and even recipes, all of which can be enjoyed not only when it's very cold outside but all year long as well. Such well-known writers as Ogden Nash, Eve Merriam, Yoshiko Uchida, and Karla Kuskin are represented, creating a diverse collection that offers something to every kind of child. Margot Tomes's black-and-white illustrations add to the appeal of each writer's work, and the book format offers a table of contents, extended booklist, and index for the reader's convenience.

Learn how to make a marshmallow snowperson and noodle snowflakes. Find out such interesting snow facts as: "Snow falls on only a third of the earth's surface, so more people have not seen snow." And, "Snow crystals always have six sides, but they are never exactly the same." Read snow folktales and enjoy the beauty of snow poems such as this one by Marie Louise Allen:

First Snow
Snow makes whiteness where it falls.
The bushes look like popcorn-balls.
And places where I always play,
Look like somewhere else today.

Program Description for
"Snowy Day: Stories and Poems"
(Show #805)

LeVar celebrates winter in "Snowy Day." Poems from the feature book—"Winter Morning" by Ogden Nash; "Snow" by Karla Kuskin; and Robert Frost's "Stopping By Woods on a Snowy Evening"—are brought to life in dramatic interpretations shot on location in Jackson Hole, Wyoming.

For the best sledding in town, LeVar and everybody else head for Gut-Flop Hill! It's a screaming good time. LeVar enjoys more classic winter fun—snowshoeing and building snow sculptures. Viewers meet someone who really loves the great outdoors—Susan Butcher, winner of the Alaskan dogsled race the Iditarod.

Science and Nature

Desert Giant: The World of the Saguaro Cactus

By Barbara Bash
Sierra Club Books/Little Brown

This beautifully detailed, excellent nonfiction book describes the life cycle of saguaro cacti, which live all over the Sonoran Desert. Realistic and colorful illustrations adorn this book, explaining all there is to know about this amazing and indispensable cactus: how it grows and the support it provides to many desert creatures. The straightforward text makes this an excellent reference book.

The saguaro cactus weighs two tons, reaches fifty feet tall, and lives up to two hundred years. It offers something to everything in the desert. Gila woodpeckers peck into its soft flesh to make room for their mate's eggs to hatch. When they move out, the elf owl, measuring only five inches long, moves in. "Because of the thin lining and the moisture stored in the saguaro's flesh, the nest stays cool even on the hottest days." At night, the long-nosed bat comes to drink the nectar hidden deep in the center of the saguaro flowers.

In June the cactus bears fruit. With it, the Tohono O'odham Indians "make jams and candies, syrups and wines . . . harvest is a time of celebration because there is good saguaro food to eat and soon the rain will come."

When the saguaro cactus eventually dies, due to old age, bacteria, strong winds, or lightning, it falls to the ground, where it slowly decomposes. This is not the end of the story, for now many insects feed off the great saguaro, and seeds sprout to become new plants. In this informative book, the circle is unbroken, and readers will find the saguaro cactus serves as a model ecosystem in the chain of desert life.

Program Description for
"Desert Giant: The World of the Saguaro Cactus"
(Show #607)

LeVar grabs his camera and sets off to explore Arizona's beautiful Sonoran Desert in "Desert Giant." He finds a saguaro cactus that's over one hundred years old—and it towers above him. A fast-paced montage catches LeVar taking souvenir pictures of himself with all kinds of cacti—a prickly subject, to be sure. A humorous look at how animals have adapted to desert life gives viewers the facts, "straight from the horse's mouth"—or jackrabbit's, as the case may be.

Herpetologist Jerry "Snakeman" Brewer takes viewers for a walk on the wild side. He finds a denning area for western diamondback rattlesnakes, and taking one of these amazing creatures in hand, points out its body parts—including its elastic skin that expands so it can swallow its prey whole. Seasons change in the desert, too, and a song montage captures moments in the sun, rain, and even snow.

Digging Up Dinosaurs

Written and illustrated by Aliki
HarperCollins

In this unique, fact-filled book, discover how dinosaur bones are
found, excavated, and reconstructed to make a dinosaur skeleton
that looks just the way it did millions and millions of years ago.
Written with amusing illustrations
and bubble text, Aliki makes this introduction to paleontology not
only approachable but extremely satisfying for dinosaur lovers of
all ages.

"Until about 200 years ago, no one knew anything about
dinosaurs. Then people began finding things in rocks. They found
large footprints. They found huge, mysterious bones and strange
teeth. People were finding fossils." These remains of plants and
animals from long ago have miraculously been preserved for fossil
hunters and scientists to find. Over the years, more and more artifacts have been discovered, cleaned, and reconstructed in museums all over the world so that we may see these awesome, ancient
creatures and better understand the way they lived on this earth.

"Dinosaurs lived millions of years ago. A few of them were as
small as birds, but most were enormous." They lived on every continent of the world. No one knows why they became extinct, but
they have not been around for 65 million years. Since the first bone
was discovered, scientists have been fascinated by the dinosaur
and seek out fossils so that they may learn more about the past and
exhibit their findings in museums for the general public. This is not

an easy job, requiring many people to locate, draw, dig, photograph, and transport the bones they find. Sometimes bones are covered with plaster to keep them from breaking during transport. Other times the skeletons are so big that the bones have to be cut apart in order to be moved!

Once at a museum, the bones are cleaned and studied. "If there are enough bones, scientists are able to build a complete skeleton. A frame is made in the shape of a dinosaur to support the bones. The bones are wired together, one by one." This takes many months to do before the dinosaur skeleton is ready for display.

"Until recently, only a few museums had dinosaurs. Then scientists learned to make copies of the skeleton." Thanks to their hard work, scientists have made it possible to see dinosaurs in museums all over the world. Bring this introductory book, filled with dinosaur facts, to the museum with you. It's bound to answer your every question.

Program Description for
"Digging Up Dinosaurs"
(Show #106)

In "Digging Up Dinosaurs," LeVar uncovers all kinds of dino-mite information. LeVar sets out in his "Jeep-a-saurus Wreck" to visit Dinosaur National Monument in Jensen, Utah. A paleontologist carefully chips away rock to reveal the skeleton of a brontosaurus who roamed the earth over 140 million years ago.

An animated dino-comic tells jokes that will make you wonder if the dinosaurs died laughing. A look at some familiar animals—elephants, rhinos, tortoises, and more—shows why these creatures can trace their family tree to some prehistoric ancestors.

Dive to the Coral Reefs

By Elizabeth Tayntor, Paul Erickson, and Les Kaufman
A New England Aquarium Book
Crown Publishers Inc.

Take an underwater dive to see a living coral reef. Vivid photographs of the rarely seen creatures make readers feel as if they are actually there. The New England Aquarium, located on Central Wharf in Boston, Massachusetts, began to build a new 186,000-gallon Caribbean Coral Reef exhibit. It sent members of the staff's

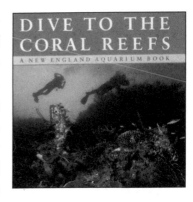

education department on an expedition to Jamaica to research coral reefs. Their findings are documented in this remarkable book, with extraordinary photographs, giving the reader an intimate look at rare coral, a moray eel, a huge sea turtle, and a host of other mysterious and intriguing sea dwellers.

Coral reefs grow in tropical oceans all over the world. A reef is an active, colorful home to millions of incredible creatures. As tall as forty feet above the sea floor or as small as a pencil eraser, coral is a living thing made up of tiny animals. The body of each coral animal, or polyp, consists of a soft, saclike wall enclosing the stomach, with a mouth surrounded by tentacles. They eat tiny plants and plankton and can live longer than five thousand years if undisturbed.

"The reef is home to literally millions of plants and animals because it offers good feeding and good places to hide. Small reef dwellers need protection from the many hunters of the reef. Larger fishes probe cracks and holes in the reef, looking for tasty crabs and worms." All sea creatures can be prey to even larger creatures such as the great barracuda or the white-tipped shark. Animals and plants are everywhere on the reef. "Here it feels like being on another planet. Enormous sponges grow out of the reef wall. Some are so large a diver can stand inside."

The coral reef is a fragile community, unable to withstand the trauma of pollution or boat propellers plowing through. In reading this book, discover the beauty of this underwater wonderland and find out how important it is that we preserve it.

Program Description for
"Dive to the Coral Reefs"
(Show #606)

LeVar goes scuba diving in the Florida Keys in "Dive to the Coral Reefs." He suits up for the dive and demonstrates the spit-swish-dunk technique that helps keep your mask clear while underwater. With diving partner Mike White, LeVar takes a walk in the ocean. The coral reefs are spectacular, teeming with brightly colored fish like the red and white parrot fish. The coral specimens are equally stunning—there are wispy sea feathers, antler-shaped elk horn coral, and brain coral that looks just like, well, a brain.

"Reef doctor" Harold Hudson repairs reefs where their natural beauty has been broken or destroyed. He and his assistant Paige show how they transplant living coral, using a special kind of cement to help it take hold in its new home. This move doesn't harm the tiny creatures that live inside the thin top skin of the coral.

Is This a House for Hermit Crab?

By Megan McDonald
Illustrated by S. D. Schindler
Orchard Books

A vulnerable hermit crab must brave the elements to find a new, bigger shell in this lovely introduction to natural science for the very young. The art, cool and gritty, blends smoothly with the text, which is told from a hermit crab's point of view. Readers will enjoy the well-paced anticipation this book provides and all but step into the pages to feel the sand between their toes.

Hermit crab is looking for a new home. He has outgrown his shell and must step along the shore, "scritch-scratch, scritch-scratch" to find the perfect abode. Nothing has fit quite right when he is tumbled into the ocean by a giant wave. The dreaded prick-lepine fish is looming nearby, so the hermit crab hides behind an empty sea snail shell. An empty shell?! Quickly, he scrambles in and is out of harm's way, having found just what he needed.

Program Description for
"Is This a House for Hermit Crab?"
(Show #1003)

LeVar builds a birdhouse in a show all about animal homes—"Is This a House for Hermit Crab?" Viewers watch nature's finest architect, the beaver, hard at work building and fortifying his dam and lodge. An adorable animation shows life inside the lodge.

Robin Leach narrates a hysterical look at "Lifestyles of the Wild and Tameless." And for an up-close view of peregrine falcons, catch a flight to New York City. Scientists scale tall buildings and bridges to keep track of these cliff-dwelling birds who have found homes amid Manhattan's skyscrapers.

Program Description for
"Seashore Surprises"
(Show #903)

Using the feature book as a reference, LeVar goes beachcombing in "Seashore Surprises." While exploring an island off the Gulf Coast of Florida, he finds beautiful shells—and even finds an animal at home inside a tulip shell.

With the help of naturalist Kristie Seaman, LeVar gets a close-up look at the tiny creatures—sea horses, shrimps, and more—that populate the eelgrass beds on the island's bay side. Lisa Satchell takes LeVar into the mangrove swamp to see the amazing ecosystem that lives in and around the roots of these unusual trees.

Koko's Kitten

By Dr. Francine Patterson
Photos by Ronald H. Cohn
Scholastic Hardcover

Everyone must wonder what animals think about. This is the true documentary of Koko, a gorilla in California, who has been taught to communicate in American Sign Language by Dr. Francine Patterson. More than anything, Koko wants a cat for her twelfth birthday. Enlightening color photographs and descriptive narrative share this historic moment in natural history when Koko requests a cat, receives and befriends it, and must mourn its untimely death.

In 1972 Penny Patterson devoted her graduate-school project to pioneering the study of animals' language abilities with Koko the gorilla as her subject. By 1985 Koko had developed a vocabulary of about five hundred words "and uses over one hundred different ones every day. She is able to communicate how she feels, what she wants, even who she is. When Koko was asked whether she was an animal or a person, Koko answered, 'Fine animal gorilla.' "

When Koko turned twelve years old, Penny asked what she'd like for her birthday. " 'Cat,' answered Koko . . . 'cat, cat, cat.' " When a litter was finally found, Koko selected a tailless tabby and named him All-Ball. The two became inseparable. "Koko did not realize that kittens don't necessarily enjoy gorilla games. Koko did understand that kittens like warmth, affection, and attention. And Koko supplied plenty."

On a foggy December morning, All-Ball was hit by a car and died instantly. Penny went to Koko immediately with the news. "Koko did not respond. I thought she didn't understand, so I left the trailer. Ten minutes later, I heard Koko cry. It was her distress call. . . . I cried too." No one was prepared for the sadness that Koko and each of her caretakers felt. But over time, Koko requested another cat, for Christmas. Her wish was granted. A red Manx cat arrived and Koko was happy. This touching chapter in Koko's life deals with love and death, openly and honestly.

Please refer to the program description for "Feelings." *Koko's Kitten* **is a Highlight Book in this episode.**

The Magic School Bus Inside the Earth

By Joanna Cole
Illustrated by Bruce Degen
Scholastic Hardcover

One of a trilogy of adventures, this is an introduction to earth science that is informative and fun. When it is time to study earth science in Ms. Frizzle's class, no one knows *what* to expect. Ms. Frizzle is known for imparting knowledge in the strangest and most unexpected ways. In this episode, we travel on the Magic School Bus to the center of the earth, learning facts every mile of the way. Comic-strip-bubble text and sidebars filled with earth anecdotes present an abundance of information.

Ms. Frizzle assigns the children in her class the task of bringing in rocks. When only four children follow through, she decides it is time to take a field trip on the Magic School Bus to learn firsthand about different kinds of rocks and the formation of the earth. The children "dig" the trip. On their first stop in a limestone cave, "we wanted to stay for a while but suddenly the bus sprouted a drill. It started boring through the rock. Frizzie shouted `Follow that bus!' And down we went." Deeper and deeper they go until they reach the earth's inner core, where it's hot, hot, hot, and later they drive straight up through a tunnel of black rock to find sky once again. Phew!

"We looked around. We had come out on an island in the middle of the ocean! 'Isn't this wonderful, class?' said Frizzie. 'We've driven right up on a volcanic island!' After collecting some rocks, it's back to the school bus they go—and just in the nick of time. The volcano's erupting! Once safely back in their classroom, they find geology was never a more interesting subject as they talk about the rocks they've collected. Take a trip with the smartest and wackiest teacher around—you'll come home with more information than you ever expected, and you'll never forget it!

Program Description for
"The Magic School Bus Inside the Earth"
(Show #701)

LeVar goes spelunking in "The Magic School Bus Inside the Earth." When he visits California Caverns in Calaveras County, California, LeVar explores the beautiful world beneath our feet. Kids guess what they think LeVar might find inside the caves. With the help of his guide Suzanne, LeVar gets a good foothold in geology.

There are waterfalls of marble, smooth as ice cream; stalactites and stalagmites; and "soda straws" of calcite—all formed by water dripping through the rock over millions of years. It's a living cave—growing at the rate of one inch per hundred years! Suzanne advises LeVar that when moving through the tight confines, it's best to walk like a caveman, with your knees bent and arms hanging low.

Storms

Written by Seymour Simon; Photos courtesy of the National Center for Atmospheric Research—National Science Foundation, the National Oceanic and Atmospheric Administration, and Richard Horodner Artwork by Frank Schwarz
Morrow Junior Books, a division of William Morrow & Co.

Award-winning science writer Seymour Simon explains everything there is to know about thunderstorms, hailstorms, lightning, tornadoes, and even hurricanes in this remarkable book for all ages. Nighttime photographs ominously display the drama of lightning crackling through the sky and hailstones as big as grapefruits! Children will be fascinated to find out more, in this book offering facts about storms and what we can do during them to stay safe and dry.

"We live at the bottom of a blanket of air called the atmosphere. The atmosphere is always moving, sometimes slowly, other times quickly and violently. These changes in the atmosphere are called the weather. We call the violent changes, storms." Annually, there are about 16 million thunderstorms around the world. Each one can drop 125 million gallons of water! Despite their danger, thunderstorms carry life-giving water from seas and lakes to dry land, cleansing our air in the process.

Lightning is a discharge of electricity within a thunderstorm. You can determine how far away lightning is striking by counting the number of seconds between the flash and the thunder. Divide this number by five. The number you get is the number of miles.

A series of photographs show a tornado rising up, whirling around, and, in less than fifteen minutes, vanishing altogether. "Tornadoes sometimes do strange things. . . . [Once a tornado] lifted a train locomotive from one track, spun it around in midair, and then set it down on another track facing in the opposite direction."

With the help of radar, satellites, and computers, we can better anticipate storms now. Nevertheless, these dramatic wonders are to be respected. Curl up on a stormy day, following the tips provided in this book, and enjoy the weather—from a distance.

Please refer to the program description for "Come A Tide."
***Storms* is a Review Book in this episode.**

Urban Roosts

Written and illustrated by Barbara Bash
Sierra Club Books/Little, Brown and Co.

Take a peek behind the scenes of a city skyline and discover the numerous birds who have learned to adapt and even thrive in this harsh environment. Inspired by a year-long study of city birds, Barbara Bash has created a masterpiece. Her brilliant watercolor illustrations are lifelike, inviting children to investigate, for themselves, the unusual world of urban ornithology.

Pigeons aren't the only birds that live in a city. As their natural habitats have been destroyed, other birds have moved here too, creating roosts in highway overpasses, on window ledges, and even in street signs. "Watch the short open pipe at the top of some traffic light poles. A pair of house sparrows may be darting in and out, bringing food to their nestlings. Sometimes you can even spot a nest in the metal casing that surrounds a traffic light. Perhaps the heat of the bulb helps keep the eggs warm."

The elusive owl finds its home under train and highway overpasses in the city but is rarely seen, for it comes out at night—hunting rats and mice to bring to its young. One of the fastest birds on earth, the peregrine falcon can be found hidden among the beams and girders of big city bridges. "People are fascinated with the peregrine falcon and are doing what they can to make this noble bird feel welcome. In many cities, people set nesting boxes filled with gravel out on skyscraper ledges. The falcons seem to like these windy, rocky heights, for they return to the boxes early each spring to lay their eggs and raise their chicks." Birds have adapted and survived with and without man's help. Treat yourself to this book and then next time you walk out on a city street, look up. You may be surprised by what you see.

Please refer to the program description for "Is This a House for Hermit Crab?" *Urban Roosts* is a Review Book in this episode.

Sports

The Bicycle Man

Written and illustrated by Allen Say
A Parnassus Press Book, published by
Houghton Mifflin Co.

THE BICYCLE MAN
by Allen Say

A group of Japanese schoolchildren are unexpectedly visited by two American soldiers, one of whom performs amazing bicycle tricks, bringing spontaneous humor and a human element to the time right after World War II. This is a true story from Allen Say's childhood, and his retelling is pure and magical. Pastel colors fill the delicate pen drawings, making this one of Mr. Say's finest works of art.

It is Sports Day at school. On this day, children, parents, teachers, and the principal compete in races and win prizes. Just as the day is ending, "a hush fell on the playground . . . two strangers were leaning over the fence and watching us. They were American soldiers. One of them was a white man with bright red hair like fire, and the other man had a face as black as the earth. They wore dark uniforms with neckties, soft caps on their heads, and red stripes on their sleeves. They had no guns."

The black man gestures to the principal that he would like to borrow his bicycle. The principal complies. Suddenly the soldier is riding the bike with the front wheel lifted off the ground, "twirling the front wheel like a spinning gyroscope." Then he rides backward! "He sat on the bicycle with his body turned around. He had to twist his neck to see where he was going. He worked his long arms and legs like a huge dancing spider. We howled with wonder." When he finishes, the entire school agrees that this was truly an amazing experience and they award the bicycle man the largest prize of the day. "Ari-ga-tow [Thank you]," says the soldier.

Program Description for

"The Bicycle Man"

(Show #703)

Wheels are the driving force in "The Bicycle Man." An animated cartoon rolls through the history of the wheel, from carts and coaches to cars and trains. LeVar tries rollerblading and gets some pointers on skateboarding from a "thrasher" named Anita. A real live bike man named Woody wheels in with freestyle cycling stunts like the "backyard."

Bikes aren't the only human-powered vehicles. There are also cars, catamarans, and rafts—even airplanes. A music video shows that wheels really do make the world go around—in pottery, planes, wheelchairs, factories, and more.

Hooray for Snail!

Written and illustrated by John Stadler
HarperCollins Trophy

The moral of this story is do not pass judgment, for sometimes the person you least expect is able to save the day. But the real fun of this book is in its simplicity. Very little text and happy, expressive illustrations make this wholesome story complete, providing an extremely satisfying read for the beginning reader.

It's Snail's turn up at bat, and grumpy Coach Hippo has given him a warning. "Snail slams the ball. The ball flies up. Snail tips his hat. The ball goes into space." We follow Snail as he hurries, at a snail's pace, all the way around the bases. The crowd anxiously looks on. Snail is so tired, he must rest at second base. The ball is coming back, Snail slides into home. Snail is safe!!

Program Description for
"The Tortoise and the Hare"
(Show #304)

(*Hooray for Snail!* is a Review Book in this episode.)

The book adaptation reprises the familiar tale of "The Tortoise and the Hare." Perseverance is the key to success, as LeVar discovers when he trains for a bike race. But along the way, LeVar has to fight off his "lazy self" if he's to do his best in the race.

Getting in shape means toning up your brain as well as your body. In karate, students learn to develop the spirit to try hard and not give up. Viewers meet children learning this Japanese art of self-defense and self-control. A music video urges athletes to give it all they've got.

Sports Pages

By Arnold Adoff
Illustrated by Steve Kuzma
HarperCollins

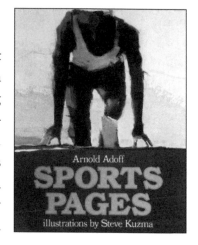

Arnold Adoff describes what it means to be an athlete in thirty-seven uniquely written poems, covering such sports as soccer, wrestling, gymnastics, running, baseball, and more. Steve Kuzma's beautiful sketches depict the grace of each sport. Each poem's text is laid out in a seemingly random but deliberate manner, adding meaning to the thought-provoking words which range in emotion from elation to disappointment. For the advanced beginning reader or as a read-aloud for avid sports lovers, this is an artful and intuitive book.

In one poem, an athlete practices every day to be the very best for himself or his team. "There is always hard work, but near the end of each final practice session, I know I am ready to do my final best. Win or lose I will do well. I am getting stronger the longer I play. I am getting better each day. I can tell."

With the elation of sports and exercise comes the occasional injury. Adoff describes the frustration that anyone who has ever been in this situation feels: "My knee is only sprained, is only swollen, and the doctor says I will be fine. I'll play again. He says that as he sits on his padded leather chair that can swivel 360 degrees. Oh why can't knees . . . ?" Whether training for a special event or for personal satisfaction, young athletes will find encouragement, empathy, and inspiration in these pages.

Program Description for
"Sports Pages"
(Show #610)

The book adaptation in "Sports Pages" is brought to life with dramatic interpretations of the poems "Watch Me on the Wing" and "Sweet." LeVar spends the day working out, and talks about the determination and emotions that go into playing sports. A music video catches athletes striving to do their personal best.

Gymnast Liz Crandall talks about what it's like to compete on the uneven bars, balance beam, and in the floor exercise. Kim and Wayne Seybold, a sister-and-brother pairs figure-skating team, share their philosophy on training: "If you think you're perfect, you don't improve"; and on attaining goals: "If you have a dream, it's always reachable."

Reading Rainbow Booklist

Programs 1–100

ABIYOYO

a story-song by Pete Seeger, illus. by Michael Hays (Macmillan Publishing Co., ISBN 0-02-781490-4)

Review Books:

BLACKBERRY INK
poems by Eve Merriam, pictures by Hans Wilhelm (William Morrow & Co., ISBN 0-688-04150-7; **lib.** ISBN 0-688-04151-5)

AYU AND THE PERFECT MOON
by David Cox (The Bodley Head/Merrimack Pub. Circle, ISBN 0-370-30533-7)

PETER AND THE WOLF
adapted from the musical tale by Sergei Prokofiev, illus. by Erna Voigt (David R. Godine, Publisher, ISBN 0-317-62883-6)

THE ADVENTURES OF TAXI DOG

by Debra and Sal Barracca, illus. by Mark Buehner (Dial Books for Young Readers, a division of Penguin Books USA, ISBN 0-8037-0671-5; **lib.** ISBN 0-8037-0672-3)

Review Books:

TAXI: A BOOK OF CITY WORDS
by Betsy and Giulio Maestro (Clarion Books: an imprint of Houghton Mifflin Co., ISBN 0-89919-528-8; **pb.** ISBN 0-395-54811-X)

I WANT A DOG
by Dayal Kaur Khalsa (Clarkson N. Potter, ISBN 0-517-56532-3)

THE FIRST DOG
by Jan Brett (Harcourt Brace, ISBN 0-15-227650-5)

ALISTAIR IN OUTER SPACE

by Marilyn Sadler, illus. by Roger Bollen (Prentice-Hall Books for

Young Readers, ISBN 0-13-022369-7; **pb.** Simon & Schuster Books for Young Readers, ISBN 0-671-68504-X)

Review Books:

CHECK IT OUT! THE BOOK ABOUT LIBRARIES
by Gail Gibbons (Harcourt Brace, ISBN 0-15-216400-6; **pb.** Voyager/HBJ, ISBN 0-15-216401-4)

COMMANDER TOAD Series
by Jane Yolen, illus. by Bruce Degen (Coward-McCann, ISBN 0-698-30744-5; **pb.** ISBN 0-698- 20620-7)

MAPS AND GLOBES
by Jack Knowlton, illus. by Harriett Barton (HarperCollins, ISBN 0-690-04457-7; **pb.** HarperCollins Trophy, ISBN 0-06-446049-5; **lib.** ISBN 0-690-04459-3)

ALISTAIR'S TIME MACHINE
by Marilyn Sadler, illus. by Roger Bollen (Simon and Schuster Books for Young Readers, ISBN 0-13-022351-4; **pb.** ISBN 0-671-68493-0)

Review Books:

FIND WALDO NOW
by Martin Handford (Little, Brown and Co., ISBN 0-316-34292-0)

THE MANY LIVES OF BENJAMIN FRANKLIN
by Aliki (Simon and Schuster Books for Young Readers, ISBN 0-671-66119-1; **pb.** ISBN 0-671-66491-3)

WHAT DOES IT DO? INVENTIONS THEN AND NOW
by Daniel Jacobs (Raintree Publishers, ISBN 0-8172-3586-8)

AMAZING GRACE
by Mary Hoffman, illus. by Caroline Binch (Dial Books for Young Readers, a division of Penguin Books USA, ISBN 0-8037-1040-2)

Review Books:

ROSES SING ON NEW SNOW: A DELICIOUS TALE
by Paul Yee, illus. by Harvey Chan (Macmillan Publishing Co.; and Groundwood Books, Canada; ISBN 0-02-793622-8)

GREAT WOMEN IN THE STRUGGLE
by Toyomi Igus, Veronica Freeman Ellis, Diane Patrick, and Valerie

Wilson Wesley (Just Us Books; **pb.** ISBN 0-940975-26-2; **lib.** ISBN 0-940975-27-0)

MIRETTE ON THE HIGH WIRE
by Emily Arnold McCully (G. P. Putnam's Sons, ISBN 0-399-22130-1)

AND STILL THE TURTLE WATCHED
by Sheila MacGill-Callahan, illus. by Barry Moser (Dial Books for Young Readers, a division of Penguin Books USA, ISBN 0-8037-0931-5)

Review Books:

THIRTEEN MOONS ON TURTLE'S BACK
by Joseph Bruchac and Jonathan London, illus. by Thomas Locker (Philomel, ISBN 0-399-22141-7)

MY FIRST GREEN BOOK: A LIFE-SIZE GUIDE TO CARING FOR OUR ENVIRONMENT
by Angela K. Wilkes (Alfred A. Knopf, ISBN 0-679-81780-8; **lib.** ISBN 0-679-91780-2)

A RIVER RAN WILD
by Lynne Cherry (Gulliver Books/Harcourt Brace, ISBN 0-15-200542-0)

ANIMAL CAFE
by John Stadler (Bradbury Press, an affiliate of Macmillan Publishing Co., ISBN 0-87888-166-2; **pb.** Aladdin, ISBN 0-689-71063-1)

Review Books:

THE MOON
by Robert Louis Stevenson, illus. by Denise Saldutti (HarperCollins, ISBN 0-06-025788-1; **pb.** HarperCollins Trophy, ISBN 0-06-443098-7; **lib.** ISBN 0-06-025789-X)

THE DREAM EATER
by Christian Garrison, illus. by Diane Goode (Bradbury Press, an affiliate of Macmillan Publishing Co., ISBN 0-87888-134-4; **pb.** Aladdin, ISBN 0-689-71058-5)

NIGHT MARKETS: BRINGING FOOD TO A CITY
by Joshua Horwitz (HarperCollins, ISBN 0-690-04378-3; **pb.**
HarperCollins Trophy, ISBN 0-06-446046-0; **lib.** ISBN 0-690-04379-1)

ARTHUR'S EYES
by Marc Brown (Atlantic Monthly Press/Little, Brown and Co., ISBN
0-316-11063-9; **pb.** ISBN 0-316-11069-8)

Review Books:

A SHOW OF HANDS
by Linda Bourke and Mary Beth Sullivan (Addison-Wesley Pub. Co.,
ISBN 0-201-07456-7; **pb.** HarperCollins Trophy, ISBN 0-06-446007-X)

THROUGH GRANDPA'S EYES
by Patricia MacLachlan, illus. by Deborah Ray (HarperCollins, ISBN
0-06-024044-Y; **pb.** HarperCollins Trophy, ISBN 0-06-443041-3; **lib.**
ISBN 0-06-024043-1)

IS THIS A BABY DINOSAUR?
by Millicent E. Selsam (HarperCollins, ISBN 0-06-025302-9; **pb.**
Scholastic, ISBN 0-06-443054-5; **lib.** ISBN 0-06-025303-7)

Highlighted Books:

ALL THE COLORS OF THE RACE
by Arnold Adoff, illus. by John Steptoe (Lothrop, Lee & Shepard
Books, ISBN 0-688-00879-8; **pb.** Beech Tree Books, ISBN 0-688-11496-2;
lib. ISBN 0-688-00880-1)

THE TURN ABOUT, THINK ABOUT, LOOK ABOUT BOOK
by Beau Gardner (Lothrop, Lee & Shepard Books, ISBN 0-688-41969-
0; **lib.** ISBN 0-688-51969-5)

ROLY GOES EXPLORING
by Philip Newth (**pb.** Philomel, ISBN 0-399-20815-1)

BARN DANCE!
by Bill Martin Jr. and John Archambault, illus. by Ted Rand (Henry
Holt and Co., ISBN 0-8050-0089-5; **pb.** Owlet Paperbacks, ISBN 0-
8050-0799-7)

Review Books:

HALF A MOON AND ONE WHOLE STAR
by Crescent Dragonwagon, illus. by Jerry Pinkney (Macmillan
Publishing Co., ISBN 0-02-733120-2; **pb.** Aladdin, an imprint of
Macmillan Publishing Co., ISBN 0-689-71415-7)

I LIKE THE MUSIC
by Leah Komaiko, illus. by Barbara Westman (HarperCollins, ISBN 0-
06-023271-4; **pb.** HarperCollins Trophy, ISBN 0-06-043189-4)

THE OLD BANJO
by Dennis Haseley, illus. by Stephen Gammell (Macmillan Publishing
Co., ISBN 0-02-743100-2; **pb.** Aladdin, an imprint of Macmillan
Publishing Co., ISBN 0-689-71380-0)

BEA AND MR. JONES

by Amy Schwartz (Bradbury Press, ISBN 0-02-781430-0; **pb.** Puffin
Books/Viking Penguin, a division of Penguin Books USA, ISBN 0-14-
050439-7)

Review Books:

MAX
by Rachel Isadora (Macmillan Publishing Co., ISBN 0-02-747450-X;
pb. Aladdin, an imprint of Macmillan Publishing Co., ISBN 0-02-
043800-1)

THERE'S A NIGHTMARE IN MY CLOSET
by Mercer Mayer (Dial Books for Young Readers, a division of
Penguin Books USA, ISBN 0-8037-8682-4; **pb.** Dial Pied Piper, a division of Penguin Books USA, ISBN 0-8037-8574-7; **lib.** ISBN 0-8037-
8683-2)

THE UGLY DUCKLING
retold by Lorinda Bryan Cauley (Harcourt Brace, ISBN 0-15-292435-3;
pb. Voyager/Harcourt Brace, ISBN 0-15-692528-1)

Highlighted Book:

DAYDREAMERS
by Eloise Greenfield, illus. by Tom Feelings (Dial Books for Young
Readers, a division of Penguin Books USA, ISBN 0-8037-2137-4; **pb.**

Dial Pied Piper, a division of Penguin Books USA, ISBN 0-8037-0167-5; **lib.** ISBN 0-8037-2134-X)

BERLIOZ THE BEAR
by Jan Brett (G.P. Putnam's Sons, a division of The Putnam & Grosset Book Group, ISBN 0-399-22248-0)

Review Books:

GEORGIA MUSIC
by Helen V. Griffith, illus. by James Stevenson (Greenwillow Books, ISBN 0-688-06071-4; **pb.** Mulberry Books, an imprint of William Morrow & Co., ISBN 0-688-09931-9; **lib.** ISBN 0-688-06072-2)

THE SCIENCE BOOK OF SOUND
by Neil Ardley, illus. by Dorling Kindersley Ltd., London (Gulliver/HBJ, ISBN 0-15-200579-X)

INTRODUCTION TO MUSICAL INSTRUMENTS SERIES: BRASS/PERCUSSION/STRINGS/WOODWINDS
by Dee Lillegard (Childrens Press, **pb.** Childrens Press)

BEST FRIENDS
by Steven Kellogg (Dial Books for Young Readers, a division of Penguin Books USA, ISBN 0-8037-0099-7; **pb.** Dial Pied Piper, a division of Penguin Books USA, ISBN 0-8037-0829-7; **lib.** ISBN 0-8037-0101-2)

Review Books:

THE STORY OF MRS. LOVEWRIGHT AND PURRLESS HER CAT
by Lore Segal, illus. by Paul O. Zelinsky (Alfred A. Knopf, ISBN 0-394-86817-X; **lib.** ISBN 0-394-96817-4)

A GIFT FOR TIA ROSA
by Karen T. Taha, illus. by Dee deRosa (Dillon Press, a division of Macmillan Publishing Co.; **pb.** Bantam Books ISBN 0-553-15978-X; **lib.** ISBN 0-87518-306-9)

THE PUPPY WHO WANTED A BOY
by Jane Thayer, illus. by Lisa McCue (William Morrow & Co., ISBN 0-688-05944-9; **pb.** Mulberry Books, an imprint of William Morrow & Co., ISBN 0-688-08293-9; **lib.** ISBN 0-688-05945-7)

THE BICYCLE MAN
by Allen Say (a Parnassus Press Book, published by Houghton Mifflin Co., ISBN 0-395-32254-5; **pb.** ISBN 0-395-50652-2)

Review Books:

THE WHITE BICYCLE
by Rob Lewis (Farrar, Straus & Giroux, ISBN 0-374-38384-7)

OUR TEACHER'S IN A WHEELCHAIR
by Mary Ellen Powers (Albert Whitman & Co.; **lib.** ISBN 0-8075-6240-8)

DELPHINE
by Molly Bang (William Morrow & Co., ISBN 0-688-05636-9; **lib.** ISBN 0-688-05637-7)

THE BIONIC BUNNY SHOW
by Marc Brown and Laurene Krasny Brown (Atlantic Monthly Press/Little, Brown and Co., ISBN 0-316-11120-1; **pb.** Little, Brown and Co., ISBN 0-316-11122-8)

Review Books:

LIGHTS! CAMERA! ACTION!
by Gail Gibbons (HarperCollins, ISBN 0-690-04476-3; **pb.** HarperCollins Trophy, ISBN 06-446088-6; **lib.** ISBN 0-690-04477-1)

THE PHILHARMONIC GETS DRESSED
by Karla Kuskin, illus. by Marc Simont (HarperCollins, ISBN 0-06-023622-1; **pb.** HarperCollins Trophy, ISBN 0-06-443124-X; **lib.** ISBN 0-06-023623-X)

RAMONA: BEHIND THE SCENES OF A TELEVISION SHOW
by Elaine Scott, photos by Margaret Miller (Morrow Junior Books, ISBN 0-688-06818-9; **pb.** Dell Yearling, ISBN 0-440-40123-2; **lib.** ISBN 0-688-06819-7)

BORED—NOTHING TO DO!
by Peter Spier (Doubleday, ISBN 0-385-13177-1; **pb.** Doubleday, ISBN 0-385-24104-6)

Review Books:

THE MAGIC WINGS: A TALE FROM CHINA
by Diane Wolkstein, illus. by Robert Andrew Parker (E.P. Dutton, a division of Penguin Books USA, ISBN 0-525-44062-3; **pb.** Dutton/Unicorn, a division of Penguin Books USA, ISBN 0-525-44275-8)

REDBIRD
an "Eyes on the Ends of Your Fingers" Book, by Patrick Fort (Orchard Books, New York; Editions Laurence Olivier Four, Caen and Chardon Bleu Editions, Lyon, France; ISBN 0-531-05746-1)

FLYING
From the "Let's Discover" Library (Raintree Publishers; **pb.** Raintree Publishers, ISBN 0-8172-2594-3; **lib.** ISBN 0-8172-2613-3)

BRINGING THE RAIN TO KAPITI PLAIN

by Verna Aardema, illus. by Beatriz Vidal (Dial Books for Young Readers, a division of Penguin Books USA, ISBN 0-8037-0809-2; **pb.** Dial Pied Piper, a division of Penguin Books USA, ISBN 0-8037-0904-8; **lib.** ISBN 0-8037-0807-6)

Review Books:

THE CLOUD BOOK
by Tomie dePaola (Holiday House, ISBN 0-8234-0259-2; **pb.** Holiday House, ISBN 0-8234-0531-1)

PETER SPIER'S RAIN
by Peter Spier (Doubleday, ISBN 0-385-15485-2; **pb.** Doubleday, ISBN 0-385-15484-4)

A STORY A STORY
by Gail E. Haley (Atheneum Publishers, an imprint of Macmillan Publishing Co., ISBN 0-689-20511-2; **pb.** Aladdin, an imprint of Macmillan Publishing Co., ISBN 0-689-71201-4)

BRUSH

by Pere Calders, illus. by Carme Solé Vendrell, trans. by Marguerite Feitlowitz (Kane/Miller Book Publishers, ISBN 0-916291-05-7; **pb.** Kane/Miller Book Publishers, ISBN 0-916291-16-2)

Review Books:

EGG-CARTON ZOO
by Rudi Haas and Hans Blohm, with an introduction by David Suzuki (**pb.** Oxford University Press, ISBN 0-19-540513-7)

WHAT THE MAILMAN BROUGHT
by Carolyn Craven, illus. by Tomie dePaola (G.P. Putnam's Sons, ISBN 0-399-21290-6)

JUMANJI
by Chris Van Allsburg (Houghton Mifflin Co., ISBN 0-395-30448-2)

BUGS

by Nancy Winslow Parker and Joan Richards Wright, illus. by Nancy Winslow Parker (Greenwillow Books, ISBN 0-688-06623-2; **pb.** Mulberry Books, an imprint of William Morrow & Co., ISBN 0-688-08296-3; **lib.** ISBN 0-688-06624-0)

Review Books:

ANT CITIES
by Arthur Dorros (HarperCollins, ISBN 0-690-04568-9; **pb.** HarperCollins Trophy, ISBN 0-06-445079-1; **lib.** ISBN 0-690-04570-0)

BACKYARD INSECTS
by Millicent E. Selsam and Ronald Goor, photos by Ronald Goor (Four Winds Press, an imprint of Macmillan Publishing Co., ISBN 0-02-781820-9; **pb.** Scholastic, ISBN 0-590-42256-1)

LADYBUG
by Barrie Watts, a Stopwatch Book (Silver Burdett Press, a division of Simon & Schuster, ISBN 0-382-09441-7; **pb.** ISBN 0-382-09960-5; **lib.** ISBN 0-382-09437-9)

Highlighted Book:

THE BUG BOOK AND THE BUG BOTTLE
by Dr. Hugh Danks, illus. by Joe Weissman (**pb.**, a Somerville House Book published by Workman Publishing, ISBN 0-89480-314-X)

A CHAIR FOR MY MOTHER

by Vera B. Williams (Greenwillow Books, ISBN 0-688-00914-X; **pb.** Mulberry Books, an imprint of William Morrow & Co., ISBN 0-688-04074-8; **lib.** ISBN 0-688-00915-8)

Review Books:

MY MAMA NEEDS ME
by Mildred Pitts Walter, illus. by Pat Cummings (Lothrop, Lee &
Shepard Books, ISBN 0-688-01670-7; **lib.** ISBN 0-688-01671-5)

I HAVE A SISTER, MY SISTER IS DEAF
by Jeanne Whitehouse Peterson, illus. by Deborah Ray
(HarperCollins, ISBN 0-06-024701-0; **pb.** HarperCollins Trophy, ISBN
0-06-443059-6; **lib.** ISBN 0-06-024702-9)

EVERETT ANDERSON'S GOODBYE
by Lucille Clifton, illus. by Ann Grifalconi (Henry Holt and Co., ISBN
0-8050-0235-9; **pb.** Owlet Paperbacks, ISBN 0-8050-0800-4)

CHICKENS AREN'T THE ONLY ONES
by Ruth Heller (Grosset & Dunlap, ISBN 0-448-01872-1; **pb.**
Sandcastle, ISBN 0-448-40454-0)

Review Books:

MRS. HUGGINS AND HER HEN HANNAH
by Lydia Dabcovich (E. P. Dutton, a division of Penguin Books USA,
ISBN 0-525-44203-0)

TURTLE AND TORTOISE
from the Animals in the Wild series by Vincent Serventy (Raintree
Publishers; **pb.** Scholastic, ISBN 0-590-40228-5; **lib.** ISBN 0-8172-2403-3)

EGG TO CHICK
by Millicent E. Selsam, illus. by Barbara Wolff (HarperCollins, ISBN
0-06-025290-1; **pb.** HarperCollins Trophy, ISBN 0-06-444113-X)

COME A TIDE
by George Ella Lyon, illus. by Stephen Gammell (Orchard Books,
ISBN 0-531-05854-9; **pb.** Orchard/Richard Jackson, ISBN 0-531-07036-0;
lib. ISBN 0-531-08454-X)

Review Books:

STORMS
by Seymour Simon (Morrow Junior Books, a division of William
Morrow & Co., ISBN 0-688-07413-8; **pb.** Mulberry Books, an imprint of
William Morrow & Co., ISBN 0-688-11708-2; **lib.** ISBN 0-688-07414-6)

TORNADO ALERT
by Franklyn M. Branley, illus. by Guilio Maestro (HarperCollins, ISBN 0-690-04686-3; **lib.** ISBN 0-690-04688-X)

WEATHER
by Rena K. Kirkpatrick, illus. by Janetta Lewin, from the Look at Science Series (Raintree Publishers, **lib.** ISBN 0-8172-2360-6)

THE DAY JIMMY'S BOA ATE THE WASH
by Trinka Hakes Noble, illus. by Steven Kellogg (Dial Books for Young Readers, a division of Penguin Books USA, ISBN 0-8037-1723-7; **pb.** Puffin/Pied Piper, a division of Penguin Books USA, ISBN 0-8037-0094-6; **lib.** ISBN 0-8037-1724-5)

Review Books:

CRICTOR
by Tomi Ungerer (HarperCollins, ISBN 0-06-026180-3; **pb.** HarperCollins Trophy, ISBN 0-06-443044-8; **lib.** ISBN 0-06-026181-1)

"COULD BE WORSE!"
by James Stevenson (Greenwillow Books, ISBN 0-688-80075-0; **pb.** Puffin Books/Viking Penguin, a division of Penguin Books USA, ISBN 0-688-07035-3; **lib.** ISBN 0-688-84075-2)

ALEXANDER AND THE TERRIBLE, HORRIBLE, NO GOOD, VERY BAD DAY
by Judith Viorst, illus. by Ray Cruz (Atheneum Publishers, an imprint of Macmillan Publishing Co., ISBN 0-689-30072-7; **pb.** Aladdin, ISBN 0-689-71173-5)

DESERT GIANT: THE WORLD OF THE SAGUARO CACTUS
by Barbara Bash (Sierra Club Books/Little, Brown and Co., ISBN 0-316-08301-1; **pb.** Sierra Club Books/Little, Brown and Co., ISBN 0-316-08307-0)

Review Books:

SNAKES ARE HUNTERS
by Patricia Lauber, illus. by Holly Keller (HarperCollins, ISBN 0-690-04628-6; **pb.** HarperCollins Trophy, ISBN 06-445080-5; **lib.** ISBN 0-690-04630-8)

CACTUS
by Cynthia Overbeck, photos by Shabo Hani, a Lerner Natural Science Book (Lerner Publications Co., ISBN 0-8225-1469-9; **pb.** First Avenue Editions, a division of Lerner Publications Co., ISBN 0-8225-9556-7; **lib.** ISBN 0-8225-1469-0)

A LIVING DESERT
by Guy J. Spencer, photos by Tim Fuller, from the "Let's Take a Trip" Series (Troll Associates, ISBN 0-8167-1169-0; **pb.** Troll Associates, ISBN 0-8167-1170-Y)

DIGGING UP DINOSAURS
by Aliki (HarperCollins, ISBN 0-690-04714-2; **pb.** HarperCollins Trophy, ISBN 0-06-445078-3; **lib.** ISBN 0-690-04716-9)

Review Books:

DINOSAUR TIME
by Peggy Parish, illus. by Arnold Lobel (HarperCollins, ISBN 0-06-024653-7; **pb.** HarperCollins Trophy, ISBN 0-06-444037-0; **lib.** ISBN 0-06-024654-5)

IF YOU ARE A HUNTER OF FOSSILS
by Byrd Baylor, illus. by Peter Parnall (Charles Scribner's Sons, ISBN 0-684-16419-1; **pb.** Aladdin, an imprint of Macmillan Publishing Co., ISBN 0-689-70773-8)

DINOSAURS! A DRAWING BOOK
by Michael Emberley (Little, Brown and Co., ISBN 0-316-23417-6; **pb.** ISBN 0-316-23631-4)

Highlighted Book:

TYRANNOSAURUS WRECKS: A BOOK OF DINOSAUR RIDDLES
by Noelle Sterne, illus. by Victoria Chess (HarperCollins, ISBN 0-690-03959-X; **pb.** HarperCollins Trophy, ISBN 0-06-443043-Y; **lib.** ISBN 0-690-03960-3)

DINOSAUR BOB AND HIS ADVENTURES WITH THE FAMILY LAZARDO
by William Joyce (HarperCollins, ISBN 0-06-023047-9; **lib.** ISBN 0-06-021584-4)

Review Books:

CASEY AT THE BAT
by Ernest Lawrence Thayer, illus. by Ken Bachaus (Raintree Publishers; **pb.** Raintree Publishers, ISBN 0-8172-2264-2; **lib.** ISBN 0-8172-2121-2)

OLD TURTLE'S BASEBALL STORIES
by Leonard Kessler (Greenwillow Books, ISBN 0-688-00723-6; **pb.** Dell Young Yearling, ISBN 0-440-40277-8; **lib.** ISBN 0-688-00724-4)

RONALD MORGAN GOES TO BAT
by Patricia Reilly Giff, illus. by Susanna Natti (Viking Kestrel, a division of Penguin Books USA, ISBN 0-670-81457-1; **pb.** Puffin Books/Viking Penguin, a division of Penguin Books USA, ISBN 0-14-050669-1)

DIVE TO THE CORAL REEFS

a New England Aquarium Book, by Elizabeth Tayntor, Paul Erickson, and Les Kaufman (Crown Publishers, ISBN 0-517-56311-8; **pb.** ISBN 0-517-58210-4)

Review Books:

HOW TO HIDE AN OCTOPUS & OTHER SEA CREATURES
from the How to Hide series by Ruth Heller (Grosset & Dunlap, ISBN 0-448-10476-8)

I CAN BE AN OCEANOGRAPHER
by Paul P. Sipiera, from the "I Can Be" Series (Children's Press, ISBN 0-516-01905-8; **pb.** ISBN 0-516-41905-6)

CREATURES OF THE SEA
by John Christopher Fine (Atheneum, an imprint of Macmillan Publishing Co., ISBN 0-689-31420-5)

DUNCAN AND DOLORES

by Barbara Samuels (Bradbury Press, an affiliate of Macmillan Publishing Co., ISBN 0-02-778210-7; **pb.** Aladdin, an imprint of Macmillan Publishing Co., ISBN 0-689-71294-4)

Review Books:

PUSS IN BOOTS
by Charles Perrault, retold and illus. by Lorinda Bryan Cauley
(Harcourt Brace, ISBN 0-15-264227-7; **pb.** Voyager/Harcourt Brace,
ISBN 0-15-264228-5)

CAT & CANARY
by Michael Foreman (Dial Books for Young Readers, a division of
Penguin Books USA, ISBN 0-8037-0137-3; **pb.** Dial Pied Piper, a division of Penguin Books USA, ISBN 0-8037-0133-0)

MOON TIGER
by Phyllis Root, illus. by Ed Young (Henry Holt and Co., ISBN 0-
8050-0896-9; **pb.** Owlet Paperbacks, ISBN 0-8050-0803-9)

FEELINGS
by Aliki (Greenwillow Books, ISBN 0-688-03831-X; **lib.** ISBN 0-688-
03832-8)

Review Books:

HONEY, I LOVE AND OTHER LOVE POEMS
by Eloise Greenfield, illus. by Diane and Leo Dillon (HarperCollins,
ISBN 0-690-01334-5; **pb.** HarperCollins Trophy, ISBN 0-06-443097-9;
lib. ISBN 0-690-03845-3)

FIREFLIES!
by Julie Brinckloe (Macmillan Publishing Co.; **pb.** Aladdin, an imprint
of Macmillan Publishing Co., ISBN 0-689-71055-0; **lib.** ISBN 0-02-
713310-9)

LOUDMOUTH GEORGE AND THE SIXTH-GRADE BULLY
by Nancy Carlson (Carolrhoda Books; **pb.** Puffin Books/Viking
Penguin, a division of Penguin Books USA, ISBN 0-14-050510-5; **lib.**
ISBN 0-87614-217-X)

Highlighted Book:

KOKO'S KITTEN
by Dr. Francine Patterson, photos by Ronald H. Cohn (Scholastic
Hardcover, an imprint of Scholastic, ISBN 0-590-33811-0; **pb.**
Scholastic, ISBN 0-590-33812-9)

FLORENCE AND ERIC TAKE THE CAKE
by Jocelyn Wild (Dial Books for Young Readers, a division of Penguin Books USA, ISBN 0-8037-0305-8)

Review Books:

UNCLE NACHO'S HAT
a bilingual Spanish/English book, adapted by Harriet Rohmer, illus. by Veg Reisberg (Children's Book Press; **lib.** ISBN 0-89239-043-3)

THE GARDEN OF ABDUL GASAZI
by Chris Van Allsburg (Houghton Mifflin Co., ISBN 0-395-27804-X)

MY FIRST COOKBOOK
by Angela Wilkes (Alfred A. Knopf, ISBN 0-394-80427-9)

FOLLOW THE DRINKING GOURD
by Jeanette Winter (Alfred A. Knopf, ISBN 0-394-89694-7; **pb.**, a Dragonfly Book, published by Alfred A. Knopf, ISBN 0-679-81997-5; **lib.** ISBN 0-394-99694-1)

Review Books:

SHAKE IT TO THE ONE THAT YOU LOVE THE BEST: PLAY SONGS AND LULLABIES FROM BLACK MUSICAL TRADITIONS
collected and adapted by Cheryl Warren Mattox, illus. from the works of Varnette P. Honeywood and Brenda Joysmith (**pb.** Warren-Mattox Productions, distributed by JTG of Nashville, ISBN 0-962-3381-0-9)

A PICTURE BOOK OF HARRIET TUBMAN
by David A. Adler, illus. by Samuel Byrd (Holiday House, ISBN 0-8234-0926-0)

SWEET CLARA AND THE FREEDOM QUILT
by Deborah Hopkinson, illus. by James Ransome (Alfred A. Knopf, ISBN 0-679-82311-5; **lib.** ISBN 0-679-92311-X)

FOX ON THE JOB
by James Marshall (Dial Books for Young Readers, a division of Penguin Books USA, ISBN 0-8037-0350-3; **pb.** ISBN 0-8037-0746-0; **lib.** ISBN 0-8037-0351-1)

Review Books:

PIG PIG GETS A JOB
by David McPhail (Dutton Children's Books, a division of Penguin
Books USA, ISBN 0-525-44619-2)

MUSIC, MUSIC FOR EVERYONE
by Vera B. Williams (Greenwillow Books, ISBN 0-688-02603-6; **pb.**
Mulberry Books, an imprint of William Morrow & Co., ISBN 0-688-
07811-7; **lib.** ISBN 0-688-02604-4)

HELPING OUT
by George Ancona (Clarion Books, an imprint of Houghton Mifflin
Co., ISBN 0-89919-278-5; **pb.** ISBN 0-395-55774-1)

THE FURRY NEWS: HOW TO MAKE A NEWSPAPER
by Loreen Leedy (Holiday House, ISBN 0-8234-0793-4)

Review Books:

GREAT NEWSPAPER CRAFTS
by F. Virginia Walter, illus. by Teddy Cameron Long (Sterling
Publishing, ISBN 0-920534-75-9; **pb.** ISBN 0-920534-79-1)

NEWSPAPERS
by David Petersen (Children's Press, ISBN 0-516-01702-0)

WHAT IT'S LIKE TO BE A . . . NEWSPAPER REPORTER
by Janet Craig, illus. by Richard Max Kolding (**pb.** Troll Associates,
ISBN 0-8167-1808-3; **lib.** ISBN 0-8167-1807-5)

GALIMOTO
by Karen Lynn Williams, illus. by Catherine Stock (Lothrop, Lee &
Shepard Books, ISBN 0-688-08789-2; **pb.** Mulberry Books, an imprint
of William Morrow & Co., ISBN 0-688-10991-8; **lib.** ISBN 0-688-08790-
6)

Review Books:

THE LITTLE PIGS' PUPPET BOOK
by N. Cameron Watson (Little, Brown and Co.; **lib.** ISBN 0-316-92468-7)

LOOK AT THIS
by Harlow Rockwell (**pb.** Aladdin, an imprint of Macmillan Publishing Co., ISBN 0-689-71165-4)

MY FIRST ACTIVITY BOOK
by Angela Wilkes (Alfred A. Knopf, ISBN 0-394-86583-9; **lib.** ISBN 0-394-96583-3)

GERMS MAKE ME SICK!
by Melvin Berger, illus. by Marylin Hafner (HarperCollins, ISBN 0-690-04428-3; **pb.** HarperCollins Trophy, ISBN 0-06-445053-8; **lib.** ISBN 0-690-04429-1)

Review Books:

THE MICROSCOPE
by Maxine Kumin, illus. by Arnold Lobel (HarperCollins, ISBN 0-06-023523-3; **pb.** HarperCollins Trophy, ISBN 0-06-443136-3; **lib.** ISBN 0-06-023524-1)

GUESS WHAT?
by Beau Gardner (Lothrop, Lee & Shepard Books, ISBN 0-688-04982-6; **lib.** ISBN 0-688-04983-4)

TEDDY BEARS CURE A COLD
by Susanna Gretz, illus. by Alison Sage (Four Winds Press, an imprint of Macmillan Publishing Co., ISBN 0-02-736960-9; **pb.** Scholastic, ISBN 0-590-42132-8)

THE GIFT OF THE SACRED DOG
by Paul Goble (Bradbury Press, an affiliate of Macmillan Publishing Co., ISBN 0-02-736560-3; **pb.** Aladdin, an imprint of Macmillan Publishing Co., ISBN 0-02-043280-1)

Review Books:

MOONSONG LULLABY
by Jamake Highwater, with photos by Marcia Keegan (Lothrop, Lee & Shepard Books, ISBN 0-688-00427-X; **lib.** ISBN 0-688-00428-8)

SUHO AND THE WHITE HORSE
retold by Yuzo Otsuka, illus. by Suekichi Akaba (Viking Penguin, a division of Penguin Books USA, ISBN 0-670-68149-0)

WHY MOSQUITOES BUZZ IN PEOPLE'S EARS
by Verna Aardema, illus. by Leo and Diane Dillon (Dial Books for
Young Readers, a division of Penguin Books USA, ISBN 0-8037-6089-2;
pb. Dial Pied Piper, a division of Penguin Books USA, ISBN 0-8037-
6088-4; **lib.** ISBN 0-8037-6087-6)

GILA MONSTERS MEET YOU AT THE AIRPORT
by Marjorie Weinman Sharmat, illus. by Byron Barton (Macmillan
Publishing Co., ISBN 0-02-782450-0; **pb.** Aladdin, an imprint of
Macmillan Publishing Co., ISBN 0-689-71383-5)

Review Books:

PETER'S CHAIR
by Ezra Jack Keats (HarperCollins, ISBN 0-06-023111-4; **pb.**
HarperCollins Trophy, ISBN 0-06-443040-5)

MITCHELL IS MOVING
by Marjorie Weinman Sharmat, illus. by Jose Aruego and Ariane
Dewey (Macmillan Publishing Co., ISBN 0-02-782410-1; **pb.** Aladdin,
an imprint of Macmillan Publishing Co., ISBN 0-02-045260-8)

THE BIG HELLO
by Janet Schulman, illus. by Lillian Hoban (Greenwillow Books, ISBN
0-688-80036-X; **pb.** Dell Yearling, ISBN 0-440-40484-3; **lib.** ISBN 0-688-
84036-I)

GREGORY, THE TERRIBLE EATER
by Mitchell Sharmat, illus. by Jose Aruego and Ariane Dewey (Four
Winds Press, an imprint of Macmillan Publishing Co., ISBN 0-02-
782250-8; **pb.** Scholastic, ISBN 0-590-40250-1)

Review Books:

MRS. PIG'S BULK BUY
by Mary Rayner (Atheneum Publishers, an imprint of Macmillan
Publishing Co., ISBN 0-689-30831-0; **pb.** Aladdin, an imprint of
Macmillan Publishing Co., ISBN 0-689-70771-1)

POEM STEW
edited by William Cole, illus. by Karen Ann Weinhaus
(HarperCollins, ISBN 0-397-31963-0; **pb.** HarperCollins Trophy, ISBN
0-06-44036-7; **lib.** ISBN 0-397-31964-9)

BETTER HOMES & GARDENS NEW JUNIOR COOK BOOK
(Meredith Corporation, ISBN 0-696-00405-4)

HILL OF FIRE

by Thomas P. Lewis, illus. by Joan Sandin (**pb.** HarperCollins Trophy, ISBN 0-06-444040-0; **lib.** ISBN 0-06-023804-6)

Review Books:

EMMA'S DRAGON HUNT
by Catherine Stock (Lothrop, Lee & Shepard Books, ISBN 0-688-02696-6; **lib.** ISBN 0-688-02698-2)

ED EMBERLEY'S SCIENCE FLIP BOOKS
by Ed Emberley (Little, Brown and Co., ISBN 0-316-23616-0)

THE TAMARINDO PUPPY AND OTHER POEMS
by Charlotte Pomerantz, illus. by Byron Barton (Greenwillow Books, ISBN 0-688-80251-6; **lib.** ISBN 0-688-82451-8)

HOT-AIR HENRY

by Mary Calhoun, illus. by Erick Ingraham (William Morrow & Co., ISBN 0-688-00501-2; **pb.** Mulberry Books, an imprint of William Morrow & Co., ISBN 0-688-04068-3; **lib.** ISBN 0-688-00502-0)

Review Books:

EASY-TO-MAKE SPACESHIPS THAT REALLY FLY
by Mary Blocksma and Dewey Blocksma, illus. by Marisabina Russo (Simon & Schuster, ISBN 0-671-66301-1; **pb.** ISBN 0-671-66302-X)

THE BIG BALLOON RACE
by Eleanor Coerr, illus. by Carolyn Croll (**pb.** HarperCollins Trophy, ISBN 0-06-444053-2; **lib.** ISBN 0-06-021353-1)

JUST US WOMEN
by Jeannette Caines, illus. by Pat Cummings (HarperCollins, ISBN 0-06-020941-0; **pb.** HarperCollins Trophy, ISBN 0-06-443056-1; **lib.** ISBN 0-06-020942-9)

HUMPHREY THE LOST WHALE: A TRUE STORY

by Wendy Tokuda and Richard Hall, illus. by Hanako Wakiyama (Heian International, ISBN 0-89346-270-5)

Review Books:

ALL ABOUT WHALES
by Dorothy Hinshaw Patent (Holiday House, ISBN 0-8234-0644-X)

WHALEWATCH!
by June Behrens, photos by John Olguin (Children's Press, **pb.** ISBN
0-516-48873-2; **lib.** ISBN 0-516-8873-4)

THE LIFE CYCLE OF THE WHALE
by Paula Z. Hogan, illus. by Karen Halt (Raintree Publishers; **lib.**
ISBN 0-8172-1500-X)

IF YOU GIVE A MOUSE A COOKIE
by Laura Joffe Numeroff, illus. by Felicia Bond (HarperCollins, ISBN
0-06-024586-7; **lib.** ISBN 0-06-024587-9)

Review Books:

THIS IS THE KEY TO THE KINGDOM
by Diane Worfolk Allison (Little, Brown and Co., ISBN 0-316-03432-0)

THE HOUSE THAT JACK BUILT
illus. by Jenny Stow (Dial Books for Young Readers, a division of
Penguin Books USA, ISBN 0-8037-1090-9)

SMART DOG
by Ralph Leemis, illus. by Chris L. Demarest (Boyds Mills Press, ISBN
1-56397-109-7)

IMOGENE'S ANTLERS
by David Small (Crown Publishers, **pb.** ISBN 0-517-56242-1; **lib.** ISBN
0-517-55564-6)

Review Books:

GEORGE SHRINKS
by William Joyce (HarperCollins, ISBN 0-06-023070-3; **pb.**
HarperCollins Trophy, ISBN 0-06-443129-0; **lib.** ISBN 0-06-023071-1)

THE TREK
by Ann Jonas (Greenwillow Books, ISBN 0-688-04799-8; **pb.** Mulberry
Books, an imprint of William Morrow & Co., ISBN 0-688-08742-6; **lib.**
ISBN 0-688-04800-5)

WHEN PANDA CAME TO OUR HOUSE
by Helen Zane Jensen (Dial Books for Young Readers, a division of Penguin Books USA, ISBN 0-8037-0236-1)

IS THIS A HOUSE FOR HERMIT CRAB?

by Megan McDonald, illus. by S. D. Schindler (Orchard Books, ISBN 0-531-05855-7; **lib.** ISBN 0-531-08455-8)

Review Books:

URBAN ROOSTS
by Barbara Bash (Sierra Club Books/Little, Brown and Co., ISBN 0-316-08306-2; **pb.** Sierra Club Books/Little, Brown and Co., ISBN 0-316-08312-7)

SPIDER'S WEB
by Christine Back and Barrie Watts, a Stopwatch book (**pb.** Silver Burdett Press, a division of Simon and Schuster, ISBN 0-382-24020-0; **lib.** ISBN 0-382-09288-0)

BUSY, BUSY SQUIRRELS
by Colleen Stanley Bare (Cobblehill Books, an affiliate of Dutton Children's Books, a division of Penguin Books USA, ISBN 0-525-65063-6)

JACK, THE SEAL AND THE SEA

by Gerald Aschenbrenner, English adaptation by Joanne Fink (Silver Burdett Press, a division of Simon & Schuster, ISBN 0-382-09735-1; **pb.** ISBN 0-671-09986-9)

Review Books:

STERLING: THE RESCUE OF A BABY HARBOR SEAL
a New England Aquarium Book, by Sandra Verrill White and Michael Filisky (Crown Publishers, ISBN 0-517-57112-9)

WATER: WHAT IT IS, WHAT IT DOES
by Judith S. Seixas, illus. by Tom Huffman (Greenwillow Books, ISBN 0-688-06607-0; **lib.** ISBN 0-688-06608-9)

A DAY IN THE LIFE OF A MARINE BIOLOGIST
by David Paige, photos by Roger Ruhlin, from the "A Day in the Life of . . ." Series (Troll Associates, ISBN 0-89375-446-3; **pb.** Troll Associates, ISBN 0-89375-447-1)

JUNE 29, 1999
by David Wiesner (Clarion Books, an imprint of Houghton Mifflin Co., ISBN 0-395-59762-5)

Review Books:

TIME TRAIN
by Paul Fleischman, illus. by Claire Ewart (A Charlotte Zolotow Book, ISBN 0-06-021709-X; **lib.** ISBN 0-06-021710-3)

GROWING VEGETABLE SOUP
by Lois Ehlert (Harcourt Brace, ISBN 0-15-232575-1; **pb.** Voyager/Harcourt Brace, ISBN 0-15-232580-8)

CLOUDY WITH A CHANCE OF MEATBALLS
by Judi Barrett, illus. by Ron Barrett (Atheneum Publishers, an imprint of Macmillan Publishing Co., ISBN 0-689-30647-4; **pb.** Aladdin, an imprint of Macmillan Publishing Co., ISBN 0-689-707495)

KATE SHELLEY AND THE MIDNIGHT EXPRESS
by Margaret K. Wetterer, illus. by Karen Ritz (Carolrhoda Books, ISBN 0-87614-425-3)

Review Books:

THE TRAIN TO LULU'S
by Elizabeth Fitzgerald Howard, illus. by Robert Casilla (Bradbury Press, an affiliate of Macmillan Publishing Co., ISBN 0-02-744620-4)

THE LITTLE ENGINE THAT COULD
by Watty Piper, illus. by George and Doris Hauman (Platt & Monk, a division of Grosset & Dunlap, ISBN 0-448-40520-2; **lib.** ISBN 0-448-13022-X)

THE POLAR EXPRESS
by Chris Van Allsburg (Houghton Mifflin Co., ISBN 0-395-38949-6)

KEEP THE LIGHTS BURNING, ABBIE
by Peter and Connie Roop, illus. by Peter E. Hanson (Carolrhoda Books; **pb.** First Avenue Editions, a division of Lerner Publications Co., ISBN 0-87614-454-7; **lib.** ISBN 0-87614-275-1)

Review Books:

VERY LAST FIRST TIME
by Jan Andrews, illus. by Ian Wallace (A Margaret K. McElderry Book, an imprint of Macmillan Publishing Co., ISBN 0-689-50388-1)

THE LITTLE RED LIGHTHOUSE AND THE GREAT GRAY BRIDGE
by Hildegarde H. Swift and Lynd Ward (Harcourt Brace, ISBN 0-15-247040-9; **pb.** Voyager/Harcourt Brace, ISBN 0-15-652840-1)

SAILING WITH THE WIND
by Thomas Locker (Dial Books for Young Readers, a division of Penguin Books USA, ISBN 0-8037-0311-2; **lib.** ISBN 0-8037-0312-0)

KNOTS ON A COUNTING ROPE

by Bill Martin Jr. and John Archambault, illus. by Ted Rand (Henry Holt and Co., ISBN 0-8050-0571-4)

Review Books:

HARRIET'S RECITAL
by Nancy Carlson (Carolrhoda Books; **pb.** Puffin Books/Viking Penguin, a division of Penguin Books USA, ISBN 0-14-050464-8; **lib.** ISBN 0-87614-181-5)

LET'S GO SWIMMING WITH MR. SILLYPANTS
by M. K. Brown (Crown Publishers; **pb.** Crown Dragonfly, ISBN 517-59030-1; **lib.** ISBN 0-517-56185-9)

OWL MOON
by Jane Yolen, illus. by John Schoenherr (Philomel Books, ISBN 0-399-21457-7)

THE LADY WITH THE SHIP ON HER HEAD

by Deborah Nourse Lattimore (Harcourt Brace, ISBN 0-15-243525-5)

Review Books:

THE FLYAWAY PANTALOONS
by Joseph Sharples, illus. by Sue Scullard (Carolrhoda Books; **pb.** First Avenue Editions, a division of Lerner Publications Co., ISBN 0-87614-527-6; **lib.** ISBN 0-87614-408-3)

AN ENCHANTED HAIR TALE
by Alexis De Veaux, illus. by Cheryl Hanna (HarperCollins, ISBN 0-

06-021623-9; **pb.** HarperCollins Trophy, ISBN 0-06-443271-8; **lib.** ISBN 0-06-021624-7)

MOOG-MOOG, SPACE BARBER
by Mark Teague (Scholastic Hardcover, an imprint of Scholastic, ISBN 0-590-43332-6; **pb.** Scholastic, ISBN 0-590-43331-8)

THE LEGEND OF THE INDIAN PAINTBRUSH
retold and illus. by Tomie dePaola (G. P. Putnam's Sons, ISBN 0-399-21534-4; **pb.** Sandcastle, ISBN 0-399-21777-0)

Review Books:

RAINBOW CROW
retold by Nancy Van Laan, illus. by Beatriz Vidal (Alfred A. Knopf, ISBN 0-394-89577-0; **pb.** Dragonfly Books, a division of Alfred A. Knopf, ISBN 0-679-81942-8; **lib.** ISBN 0-394-99577-5)

INDIANS OF THE AMERICAS
from the New True Book Series (Children's Press)

THE MUD PONY
retold by Caron Lee Cohen, illus. by Shonto Begay (Scholastic Hardcover, an imprint of Scholastic, ISBN 0-590-41525-5; **pb.** Scholastic, ISBN 0-590-41526-3)

LIANG AND THE MAGIC PAINTBRUSH
by Demi (Henry Holt and Co., ISBN 0-8050-0220-0; **pb.** Owlet Paperbacks, ISBN 0-8050-0801-2)

Review Books:

EMMA
by Wendy Kesselman, illus. by Barbara Cooney (Doubleday, ISBN 0-385-13461-4; **pb.** HarperCollins Trophy, ISBN 0-06-443077-4)

BEN'S TRUMPET
by Rachel Isadora (Greenwillow Books, ISBN 0-688-80194-3; **pb.** Mulberry Books, an imprint of William Morrow & Co., ISBN 0-688-10988-8)

IF YOU TAKE A PENCIL
by Fulvio Testa (Dial Books for Young Readers, a division of Penguin

Books USA, ISBN 0-8037-4023-9; **pb.** Dial Pied Piper, a division of Penguin Books USA, ISBN 0-8037-0165-9)

THE LIFE CYCLE OF THE HONEYBEE
by Paula Z. Hogan, illus. by Geri K. Strigenz (Raintree Publishers, ISBN 0-8172-1256-6)

Review Books:

THE REASON FOR A FLOWER
by Ruth Heller (Grosset & Dunlap, ISBN 0-448-14495-6)

THE LADY AND THE SPIDER
by Faith McNulty, illus. by Bob Marstall (HarperCollins, ISBN 0-06-024191-8; **pb.** HarperCollins Trophy, ISBN 0-06-443152-5; **lib.** ISBN 0-06-024192-6)

GOING BUGGY! JOKES ABOUT INSECTS
by Peter and Connie Roop, illus. by Joan Hanson (Lerner Publications Co.; **pb.** First Avenue Editions, a division of Lerner Publications Co., ISBN 0-8225-9530-3; **lib.** ISBN 0-8225-0988-1)

LITTLE NINO'S PIZZERIA
by Karen Barbour (Harcourt Brace, ISBN 0-15-247650-4; **pb.** Voyager/Harcourt Brace, ISBN 0-15-246321-6)

Review Books:

EATS POEMS
by Arnold Adoff, illus. by Susan Russo (Lothrop, Lee and Shepard Books, ISBN 0-688-41901-1; **pb.** Mulberry Books, an imprint of William Morrow & Co., ISBN 0-688-11695-7; **lib.** ISBN 0-688-51901-6)

WHAT HAPPENS TO A HAMBURGER
by Paul Showers, illus. by Anne Rockwell (HarperCollins, ISBN 0-690-04426-7; **pb.** HarperCollins Trophy, ISBN 0-06-445013-9; **lib.** ISBN 0-690-04427-5)

THE POPCORN BOOK
by Tomie dePaola (Holiday House, ISBN 0-8234-0314-9; **pb.** Holiday House, ISBN 0-8234-0533-8)

LOUIS THE FISH

by Arthur Yorinks, illus. by Richard Egielski (Farrar, Straus & Giroux, ISBN 0-374-34658-5; **pb.** Farrar, Straus & Giroux, ISBN 0-374-44598-2)

Review Books:

WHERE THE WILD THINGS ARE
by Maurice Sendak (HarperCollins, ISBN 0-06-025520-X; **pb.** HarperCollins Trophy, ISBN 0-06-443178-9; **lib.** ISBN 0-06-225521-8)

A FISH HATCHES
by Joanna Cole and Jerome Wexler (William Morrow & Co., ISBN 0-688-22153-X; **lib.** ISBN 0-688-32153-4)

ONE MONDAY MORNING
by Uri Shulevitz (Charles Scribner's Sons, ISBN 0-684-13195-1; **pb.** Aladdin, ISBN 0-689-71062-3)

LUDLOW LAUGHS

by Jon Agee (Farrar, Straus & Giroux, ISBN 0-374-34666-6; **pb.** a Sunburst Book/Farrar, Straus & Giroux, ISBN 0-374-44663-6)

Review Books:

PIG WILLIAM
by Arlene Dubanevich (Bradbury Press, an affiliate of Macmillan Publishing Co., ISBN 0-02-733200-4; **pb.** Aladdin, ISBN 0-689-71372-X)

SHAKE MY SILLIES OUT
a Raffi Song to Read, illus. by David Allender (Crown Publishers, ISBN 0-517-56646-X; **pb.** ISBN 0-517-56647-8)

THE MAKE ME LAUGH! JOKE BOOKS
a series illus. by Joan Hanson (Lerner Publications Co.; **pb.** First Avenue Editions, a division of Lerner Publications Co.)

THE MAGIC SCHOOL BUS INSIDE THE EARTH

by Joanna Cole, illus. by Bruce Degen (Scholastic Hardcover, ISBN 0-590-40759-7; **pb.** Scholastic, ISBN 0-590-40760-0)

Review Books:

CAVES
by Roma Gans, illus. by Giulio Maestro (HarperCollins, ISBN 0-690-01070-2)

HOW TO DIG A HOLE TO THE OTHER SIDE OF THE WORLD
by Faith McNulty, illus. by Marc Simont (HarperCollins, ISBN 0-06-024147-0; **pb.** HarperCollins Trophy, ISBN 0-06-443218-1; **lib.** ISBN 0-06-024148-9)

ROCK COLLECTING
by Roma Gans, illus. by Holly Keller (HarperCollins, ISBN 0-690-04265-5; **pb.** HarperCollins Trophy, ISBN 0-06-445063-5; **lib.** ISBN 0-690-04266-3)

MAMA DON'T ALLOW
by Thacher Hurd (HarperCollins, ISBN 0-06-022689-7; **pb.** HarperCollins Trophy, ISBN 0-06-443078-2; **lib.** ISBN 0-06-022690-0)

Review Books:

MIRANDA
by Tricia Tusa (Macmillan Publishing Co., ISBN 0-02-789520-3; **pb.** Aladdin, an imprint of Macmillan Publishing Co., ISBN 0-689-71064-X)

APT. 3
by Ezra Jack Keats (Macmillan Publishing Co., ISBN 0-02-749510; **pb.** Aladdin, an imprint of Macmillan Publishing Co., ISBN 0-689-71059-3)

ALLIGATOR SHOES
by Arthur Dorros (**pb.** Dutton/Unicorn, a division of Penguin Books USA, ISBN 0-525-44428-9)

Highlighted Book:

MOUTHSOUNDS
by Frederick R. Newman (**pb.** Workman Publishing, ISBN 0-89480-128-7)

MEANWHILE BACK AT THE RANCH
by Trinka Hakes Noble, illus. by Tony Ross (Dial Books for Young Readers, a division of Penguin Books USA, ISBN 0-8037-0353-8; **lib.** ISBN 0-8037-0354-6)

Review Books:

DAKOTA DUGOUT
by Ann Turner, illus. by Ronald Himler (Macmillan Publishing Co., ISBN 0-02-789700-1; **pb.** Aladdin, an imprint of Macmillan Publishing Co., ISBN 0-689-71296-0)

BOSSYBOOTS
by David Cox (Crown Publishers, ISBN 0-517-56491-2)

RODEO
by Cheryl Walsh Bellville (Carolrhoda Books, **pb.** First Avenue Editions, a division of Lerner Publications Co., ISBN 0-87614-492-X; **lib.** ISBN 0-87614-272-2)

THE MILK MAKERS
by Gail Gibbons (Macmillan Publishing Co., ISBN 0-02-736640-5; **pb.** Aladdin, an imprint of Macmillan Publishing Co., ISBN 0-689-71116-6)

Review Books:

BABY ANIMALS ON THE FARM
by Hans-Heinrich Isenbart, photos by Ruth Rau, trans. by Elizabeth D. Crawford (G. P. Putnam's Sons, ISBN 0-399-20960-3)

WHALES AND OTHER SEA MAMMALS
by Elsa Posell (Children's Press, ISBN 0-516-01663-6; **pb.** Children's Press, ISBN 0-516-41663-4)

FROM BLOSSOM TO HONEY
a "Start to Finish" Book by Ali Mitgutsch (Carolrhoda Books; **lib.** ISBN 0-87614-146-7)

MISS NELSON IS BACK
by Harry Allard and James Marshall, illus. by James Marshall (Houghton Mifflin Co., ISBN 0-395-41668-X; **pb.** Houghton Mifflin Co., ISBN 0-590-33467-0; **lib.** ISBN 0-395-32956-6)

Review Books:

GRANDMAMA'S JOY
by Eloise Greenfield, illus. by Carole Byard (Philomel Books, ISBN 0-529-05536-8; **lib.** ISBN 0-529-05537-6)

DADDY IS A MONSTER SOMETIMES
by John Steptoe (HarperCollins, ISBN 0-397-31762-X; **pb.**
HarperCollins Trophy, ISBN 0-06-443042-1; **lib.** ISBN 0-397-31893-6)

HARLEQUIN AND THE GIFT OF MANY COLORS
by Remy Charlip and Burton Supree (Four Winds Press, an imprint of
Macmillan Publishing Co., ISBN 0-8193-0494-8; **lib.** ISBN 0-8193-0495-6)

Highlighted Book:

THE UPSIDE DOWN RIDDLE BOOK
riddles compiled and edited by Louis Phillips, Upside Down
Graphics by Beau Gardner (Lothrop, Lee & Shepard Books, ISBN 0-
688-00931-X; **lib.** ISBN 0-688-00932-8)

MRS. KATZ AND TUSH
by Patricia Polacco (a Bantam Little Rooster Book, ISBN 0-553-08122-5)

Review Books:

ABUELA
by Arthur Dorros, illus. by Elisa Kleven (Dutton Children's Books, a
division of Penguin Books USA, ISBN 0-525-44750-4)

WILFRID GORDON MCDONALD PARTRIDGE
by Mem Fox, illus. by Julie Vivas (American edition by Kane/Miller,
ISBN 0-949641-16-2; **pb.** ISBN 0-916291-26-X)

KWANZAA
by Deborah Newton Chocolate, illus. by Melodye Rosáles (Children's
Press, ISBN 0-516-03991-1; **pb.** ISBN 0-516-43991-X)

MUFARO'S BEAUTIFUL DAUGHTERS
by John Steptoe (Lothrop, Lee & Shepard Books, ISBN 0-688-04045-4;
lib. ISBN 0-688-04046-2)

Review Books:

WHO'S IN RABBIT'S HOUSE?
by Verna Aardema, illus. by Leo and Diane Dillon (Dial Books for
Young Readers, a division of Penguin Books USA, ISBN 0-8037-9550-5;

pb. Dial Pied Piper, a division of Penguin Books USA, ISBN 0-8037-9549-1; **lib.** ISBN 0-8037-9551-3)

JAMBO MEANS HELLO: SWAHILI ALPHABET BOOK
by Muriel Feelings, illus. by Tom Feelings (Dial Books for Young Readers, a division of Penguin Books USA, ISBN 0-8037-4346-7; **pb.** Dial Pied Piper, a division of Penguin Books USA, ISBN 0-8037-4428-5; **lib.** ISBN 0-8037-4350-5)

JAFTA Series
by Hugh Lewin, illus. by Lisa Kopper (Carolrhoda Books; **pb.** First Avenue Editions, a division of Lerner Publications Co.)

MUMMIES MADE IN EGYPT
by Aliki (HarperCollins, ISBN 0-690-03858-5; **pb.** HarperCollins Trophy, ISBN 0-06-446011-8; **lib.** ISBN 0-690-03859-3)

Review Books:

BILL AND PETE GO DOWN THE NILE
by Tomie dePaola (G. P. Putnam's Sons, ISBN 0-399-21395-3; **pb.** ISBN 0-399-22003-8)

I CAN BE AN ARCHAEOLOGIST
by Robert B. Pickering, from the "I Can Be" Series (Children's Press; **pb.** ISBN 0-516-41909-9; **lib.** ISBN 0-516-01909-0)

VISITING THE ART MUSEUM
by Laurene Krasny Brown and Marc Brown (E. P. Dutton, a division of Penguin Books USA, ISBN 0-525-44233-2; **pb.** Dutton/Unicorn, a division of Penguin Books USA, ISBN 0-525-44568-4)

MY LITTLE ISLAND
by Frané Lessac (HarperCollins, ISBN 0-397-32114-7; **pb.** HarperCollins Trophy, ISBN 0-06-443146-0; **lib.** ISBN 0-397-32115-5)

Review Books:

YAGUA DAYS
by Cruz Martel, illus. by Jerry Pinkney (Dial Books for Young Readers, a division of Penguin Books USA, ISBN 0-8037-9765-6; **pb.**

Dial Pied Piper, a division of Penguin Books USA, ISBN 0-8037-0457-7; **lib.** ISBN 0-8037-9766-4)

NICHOLAS BENTLEY STONINGPOT III
by Ann McGovern, illus. by Tomie dePaola (Boyds Mills Press, ISBN 1-56397-104-6)

THE VIKING CHILDREN'S WORLD ATLAS
by Jacqueline Tivers and Michael Day (Viking Kestrel, a division of Penguin Books USA, ISBN 0-670-21791-3; **pb.** Puffin, ISBN 0-14-031874-7)

MYSTERY ON THE DOCKS
by Thacher Hurd (HarperCollins, ISBN 0-06-022701-X; **pb.** HarperCollins Trophy, ISBN 0-06-443058-8; **lib.** ISBN 0-06-022702-8)

Review Books:

BIG CITY PORT
by Betsy Maestro and Ellen DelVecchio, illus. by Giulio Maestro (Four Winds Press, an imprint of Macmillan Publishing Co., ISBN 0-590-07869-0; **pb.** Scholastic, ISBN 0-590-41577-8; **lib.** ISBN 0-02-462110-3)

THE WRECK OF THE ZEPHYR
by Chris Van Allsburg (Houghton Mifflin Co.; **lib.** ISBN 0-395-33075-0)

NATE THE GREAT Mystery Series
by Marjorie Weinman Sharmat, illus. by Marc Simont (Coward-McCann; **pb.** Dell Yearling)

OPT: AN ILLUSIONARY TALE
by Arline and Joseph Baum (Viking Penguin, a division of Penguin Books USA, ISBN 0-670-80870-9; **pb.** Puffin Books/Viking Penguin, a division of Penguin Books USA, ISBN 0-14-050573-3)

Review Books:

LENSES! TAKE A CLOSER LOOK
by Siegfried Aust, illus. by Helge Nyncke (Lerner Publications Co., ISBN 0-8225-2151-2)

HIDE AND SEEK
edited by Jennifer Coldrey and Karen Goldie-Morrison, an Oxford
Scientific Films Book (G. P. Putnam's Sons, ISBN 0-399-21342-2)

IF AT FIRST YOU DO NOT SEE
by Ruth Brown (Henry Holt and Co., ISBN 0-8050-1053-X; **pb.** ISBN
0-8050-1031-9)

OX-CART MAN
by Donald Hall, illus. by Barbara Cooney (Viking Penguin, a division
of Penguin Books USA, ISBN 0-670-53328-9; **pb.** Puffin Books/Viking
Penguin, a division of Penguin Books USA, ISBN 0-14-050441-9; **lib.**
ISBN 0-670-53328-9)

Review Books:

ROUND TRIP
by Ann Jonas (Greenwillow Books, ISBN 0-688-01772-X; **pb.**
Scholastic, ISBN 0-590-40956-5; **lib.** ISBN 0-688-01781-9)

A WINTER PLACE
by Ruth Yaffe Radin, illus. by Mattie Lou O'Kelley (Little, Brown and
Co., ISBN 0-316-73218-4; **pb.** ISBN 0-316-73219-2; **lib.** ISBN 0-316-
73218-4)

WAGON WHEELS
by Barbara Brenner, illus. by Don Bolognese (HarperCollins, ISBN 0-
06-020668-3; **pb.** HarperCollins Trophy, ISBN 0-06-444052-4; **lib.** ISBN
0-06-020669-1)

THE PAPER CRANE
by Molly Bang (Greenwillow Books, ISBN 0-688-04108-6; **pb.**
Mulberry Books, an imprint of William Morrow & Co., ISBN 0-688-
07333-6; **lib.** ISBN 0-688-04109-4)

Review Books:

HOW MY PARENTS LEARNED TO EAT
by Ina R. Friedman, illus. by Allen Say (Houghton Mifflin Co.; **pb.**
Sandpiper, ISBN 0-395-44235-4; **lib.** ISBN 0-395-35379-3)

"PAPER" THROUGH THE AGES
by Shaaron Cosner, illus. by Priscilla Kiedrowski (Carolrhoda Books; **lib.** ISBN 0-87614-270-6)

PERFECT CRANE
by Anne Laurin, illus. by Charles Mikolaycak (HarperCollins, ISBN 0-06-023743-0; **pb.** HarperCollins Trophy, ISBN 0-06-443154-1; **lib.** ISBN 0-06-023744-9)

Highlighted Book:

EASY ORIGAMI
by Dokuohtei Nakano, trans. by Eric Kenneway (Viking Kestrel, a division of Penguin Books USA, ISBN 0-670-80382-0)

THE PATCHWORK QUILT
by Valerie Flournoy, illus. by Jerry Pinkney (Dial Books for Young Readers, a division of Penguin Books USA, ISBN 0-8037-0097-0; **lib.** ISBN 0-8037-0098-9)

Review Books:

THE TWO OF THEM
by Aliki (Greenwillow Books, ISBN 0-688-80225-7; **lib.** ISBN 0-688-84225-9)

ANGEL CHILD, DRAGON CHILD
by Michelle Maria Surat, illus. by Vo-Dinh Mai (Carnival Press/Raintree Publishers; **pb.** Scholastic, ISBN 0-590-42271-5; **lib.** ISBN 0-940742-12-8)

BEING ADOPTED
by Maxine B. Rosenberg, photos by George Ancona (Lothrop, Lee & Shepard Books, ISBN 0-688-02672-9; **lib.** ISBN 0-688-02673-7)

PAUL BUNYAN
retold and illus. by Steven Kellogg (William Morrow & Co., ISBN 0-688-03849-2; **pb.** Mulberry Books, an imprint of William Morrow & Co., ISBN 0-688-05800-0; **lib.** ISBN 0-688-03850-6)

Review Books:

THE STAR-SPANGLED BANNER
illus. by Peter Spier (Doubleday, ISBN 0-385-09458-2; **pb.** ISBN 0-385-23401-5; **lib.** ISBN 0-385-07746-7)

THE LEGEND OF THE BLUEBONNET
retold and illus. by Tomie dePaola (G. P. Putnam's Sons, ISBN 0-399-20937-9; **pb.** ISBN 0-399-20938-7)

WHALE IN THE SKY
by Anne Siberell (E. P. Dutton, a division of Penguin Books USA, ISBN 0-525-44021-6; **pb.** Dutton/Unicorn, a division of Penguin Books USA, ISBN 0-525-44197-2)

PERFECT THE PIG
by Susan Jeschke (Henry Holt and Co., ISBN 0-8050-0704-0; **pb.** Scholastic, ISBN 0-590-33741-6)

Review Books:

POINSETTIA & HER FAMILY
by Felicia Bond (HarperCollins, ISBN 0-690-04144-6; **pb.** HarperCollins Trophy, ISBN 0-06-443076-6; **lib.** ISBN 0-690-04145-4)

THE BIONIC BUNNY SHOW
by Marc Brown and Laurene Krasny Brown (Atlantic Monthly Press/Little, Brown and Co., ISBN 0-316-11120-1; **pb.** Little, Brown and Co., ISBN 0-316-11122-8)

HECTOR, THE ACCORDION-NOSED DOG
by John Stadler (Bradbury Press, an affiliate of Macmillan Publishing Co., ISBN 0-02-786680-7; **pb.** Aladdin, an imprint of Macmillan Publishing Co., ISBN 0-02-688763-0)

Highlighted Book:

THE BOOK OF PIGERICKS
by Arnold Lobel (HarperCollins, ISBN 0-06-023982-4; **pb.** HarperCollins Trophy, ISBN 0-06-443163-0; **lib.** ISBN 0-06-023983-2)

THE PIGGY IN THE PUDDLE
by Charlotte Pomerantz, illus. by James Marshall (Macmillan Publishing Co., ISBN 0-02-774900-2; **pb.** Aladdin, an imprint of Macmillan Publishing Co., ISBN 0-689-71293-6)

Review Books:

OINK
by Arthur Geisert (Houghton Mifflin Co., ISBN 0-395-55329-6)

THE HIPPOPOTAMUS SONG: A MUDDY LOVE STORY
by Michael Flanders and Donald Swann, illus. by Nadine Bernard
Westcott (Joy Street/Little, Brown and Co., ISBN 0-316-28557-9)

THIS HOUSE IS MADE OF MUD
by Ken Buchanan, illus. by Libba Tracy (Northland Publishing Co.,
ISBN 0-87358-518-6)

THE PURPLE COAT
by Amy Hest, illus. by Amy Schwartz (Four Winds Press, an imprint
of Macmillan Publishing Co., ISBN 0-02-743640-3; **pb.** Aladdin, an
imprint of Macmillan Publishing Co., ISBN 0-689-71634-6)

Review Books:

PABLO PICASSO
by Ibi Lepscky, illus. by Paolo Cardoni, trans. by Howard Rodger
MacLean (Barron's Educational Series, ISBN 0-8120-5511-X)

THE GOAT IN THE RUG
by Charles L. Blood and Martin Link, illus. by Nancy Winslow Parker
(Four Winds Press, an imprint of Macmillan Publishing Co., ISBN 0-
02-710920-8; **pb.** Aladdin, an imprint of Macmillan Publishing Co.,
ISBN 0-689-71418-1)

HOW A BOOK IS MADE
by Aliki (HarperCollins, ISBN 0-690-04496-8; **pb.** HarperCollins
Trophy, ISBN 0-06-446085-1; **lib.** ISBN 0-690-04498-4)

RACCOONS AND RIPE CORN/DEER AT THE BROOK/COME OUT, MUSKRATS
by Jim Arnosky (Lothrop, Lee & Shepard Books, ISBN 0-688-05455-
2/0-688-04099-3/0-688-05457-9; **pb.** Mulberry Books, an imprint of
William Morrow & Co., ISBN 0-688-10489-4/0-688-10488-6/0-688-
10490-8)

Review Books:

BIRD WATCH
by Jane Yolen, illus. by Ted Lewin (Philomel Books, ISBN 399-21612-X)

MY FIRST NATURE BOOK
by Angela Wilkes (Alfred A. Knopf, ISBN 0-394-86610-X; **lib.** ISBN 0-
394-96610-4)

TREE TRUNK TRAFFIC
by Bianca Lavies (Dutton Children's Books, a division of Penguin Books USA, ISBN 0-525-44495-5; **pb.** Puffin Unicorn, ISBN 0-14-054837-8)

RECHENKA'S EGGS
by Patricia Polacco (Philomel Books, a division of the Putnam & Grosset Book Group, ISBN 0-399-21501-8)

Review Books:

THE TALKING EGGS
by Robert D. San Souci, illus. by Jerry Pinkney (Dial Books for Young Readers, a division of Penguin Books USA, ISBN 0-8037-0619-7; **lib.** ISBN 0-8037-0620-0)

STEFAN & OLGA
by Betsy Day (Dial Books for Young Readers, a division of Penguin Books USA, ISBN 0-8037-0816-5; **lib.** ISBN 0-8037-0817-3)

I MADE IT MYSELF
by Sabine Lohf (Children's Press, ISBN 0-516-09254-5; **pb.** Children's Press, ISBN 0-516-49254-3)

THE ROBBERY AT THE DIAMOND DOG DINER
by Eileen Christelow (Clarion Books, an imprint of Houghton Mifflin Co., ISBN 0-89919-425-7; **pb.** ISBN 0-317-69509-6)

Review Books:

AUNT EATER LOVES A MYSTERY
by Doug Cushman (HarperCollins, ISBN 0-06-021326-4; **pb.** HarperCollins Trophy, ISBN 0-06-444126-1; **lib.** ISBN 0-06-021327-2)

A CACHE OF JEWELS AND OTHER COLLECTIVE NOUNS
by Ruth Heller (Grosset & Dunlap, ISBN 0-448-19211-X; **pb.** ISBN 0-448-40075-8)

BETTER HOMES & GARDENS STEP-BY-STEP KIDS' COOK BOOK
(Meredith Corporation, ISBN 0-696-01325-8; **pb.** ISBN 0-696-01327-4)

RUMPELSTILTSKIN

retold and illus. by Paul O. Zelinsky (E. P. Dutton, a division of Penguin Books USA, ISBN 0-525-44265-0)

Review Books:

A MEDIEVAL FEAST
by Aliki (HarperCollins, ISBN 0-690-04245-0; **pb.** HarperCollins Trophy, ISBN 0-06-446050-9; **lib.** ISBN 0-690-04246-9)

THE STORY OF A CASTLE
by John S. Goodall (A Margaret K. McElderry Book, an imprint of Macmillan Publishing Co., ISBN 0-689-50405-5)

THE SLEEPING BEAUTY
retold and illus. by Mercer Mayer (Macmillan Publishing Co., ISBN 0-02-765340-4)

THE RUNAWAY DUCK

by David Lyon (Lothrop, Lee & Shepard Books, ISBN 0-688-04002-0; **pb.** Mulberry Books, an imprint of William Morrow & Co., ISBN 0-688-07334-4; **lib.** ISBN 0-688-04003-9)

Review Books:

DABBLE DUCK
by Anne Leo Ellis, illus. by Sue Truesdell (HarperCollins, ISBN 0-06-021817-7; **pb.** HarperCollins Trophy, ISBN 0-06-443153-3)

THE STORY ABOUT PING
by Marjorie Flack and Kurt Wiese (Viking Kestrel, a division of Penguin Books USA; **pb.** Puffin Books/Viking Penguin, a division of Penguin Books USA, ISBN 0-14-050241-6; **lib.** ISBN 0-670-67223-8)

JAMAICA'S FIND
by Juanita Havill, illus. by Anne Sibley O'Brien (Houghton Mifflin Co., ISBN 0-395-39376-0; **pb.** ISBN 0-395-45357-7)

THE SALAMANDER ROOM

by Anne Mazer, illus. by Steve Johnson (Alfred A. Knopf, ISBN 0-394-82945-X; **lib.** ISBN 0-394-92945-4)

Review Books:

THE GREAT KAPOK TREE: A TALE OF THE AMAZON RAIN FOREST
by Lynne Cherry (Gulliver Books/Harcourt Brace, ISBN 0-15-200520-X)

CHIPMUNK SONG
by Joanne Ryder, illus. by Lynne Cherry (Lodestar Books, an affiliate of Dutton Children's Books, a division of Penguin Books USA, ISBN 0-525-67191-9; **pb.** ISBN 0-525-67312-1)

FROGS, TOADS, LIZARDS AND SALAMANDERS
by Nancy Winslow Parker and Joan Richards Wright, illus. by Nancy Winslow Parker (Greenwillow Books, ISBN 0-688-08680-2;, ISBN **lib.** 0-688-08681-0)

SAM THE SEA COW
by Francine Jacobs, illus. by Laura Kelly (Walker and Co., ISBN 0-8027-8147-0; **pb.** ISBN 0-8027-7373-7)

Review Books:

MANATEES
by Emilie U. Lepthien (Children's Press **lib.** ISBN 0-516-01114-6; **pb.** ISBN 0-516-41114-4)

"10 THINGS I KNOW" BOOKS
by Wendy Wax and Della Rowland, illus. by Thomas Payne (Calico Books, an imprint of Contemporary Books)

WILL WE MISS THEM? ENDANGERED SPECIES
by Alexandra Wright, illus. by Marshall Peck III (Charlesbridge Publishing, ISBN 0-88106-489-0; **pb.** ISBN 0-88106-448-2)

SEASHORE SURPRISES
by Rose Wyler, illus. by Steven James Petruccio (Julian Messner, an imprint of Simon & Schuster Children's Book Division, ISBN 0-671-69165-1; **pb.** ISBN 0-671-69167-8)

Review Books:

IS THIS A HOUSE FOR HERMIT CRAB?
by Megan McDonald, illus. by S. D. Schindler (Orchard Books, ISBN 0-531-05855-7; **lib.** ISBN 0-531-08455-8)

THE SEASHORE BOOK
by Charlotte Zolotow, illus. by Wendell Minor (HarperCollins, ISBN 0-06-020213-0; **lib.** ISBN 0-06-020214-9)

WHAT'S INSIDE? SHELLS
by Angela Royston, photos by Andreas von Einsiedel (Dorling Kindersley, Inc., ISBN 1-879431-10-6)

SILENT LOTUS

by Jeanne M. Lee (Farrar, Straus & Giroux, ISBN 0-374-36911-9)

Review Books:

THE HANDMADE ALPHABET
by Laura Rankin (Dial Books for Young Readers, a division of Penguin Books USA, ISBN 0-8037-0974-9; **lib.** ISBN 0-8037-0975-7)

HAND RHYMES
collected and illus. by Marc Brown (Dutton Children's Books, a division of Penguin Books USA, ISBN 0-525-44201-4; **pb.** Puffin Unicorn, a division of Penguin Books USA, ISBN 0-14-054939-0)

AMY: THE STORY OF A DEAF CHILD
by Lou Ann Walker, photos by Michael Abramson (Lodestar Books, an affiliate of Dutton Children's Books, a division of Penguin Books USA, ISBN 0-525-67145-5)

SIMON'S BOOK

by Henrik Drescher (Lothrop, Lee & Shepard Books, ISBN 0-688-02085-2; **pb.** Scholastic, ISBN 0-590-41934-X; **lib.** ISBN 0-688-02086-0)

Review Books:

BEGIN AT THE BEGINNING
by Amy Schwartz (HarperCollins, ISBN 0-06-025227-8; **pb.** HarperCollins Trophy, ISBN 0-06-443060-X; **lib.** ISBN 0-06-025228-6)

WHAT'S UNDER MY BED?
by James Stevenson (Greenwillow Books, ISBN 0-688-02325-8; **pb.** Puffin Books/Viking Penguin, a division of Penguin Books USA, ISBN 0-14-050485-0; **lib.** ISBN 0-688-02327-4)

ME AND NEESIE
by Eloise Greenfield, illus. by Moneta Barnett (HarperCollins, ISBN 0-690-00714-0; **pb.** HarperCollins Trophy, ISBN 0-06-443057-X; **lib.** ISBN 0-690-00715-9)

SNOWY DAY: STORIES AND POEMS
edited by Caroline Feller Bauer, illus. by Margot Tomes
(HarperCollins, ISBN 0-397-32176-7; **pb.** HarperCollins Trophy, ISBN
0-06-446123-8; **lib.** ISBN 0-397-32177-5)

Review Books:

WINTER
by Ron Hirschi, photos by Thomas D. Mangelsen (Cobblehill Books,
an affiliate of Dutton Children's Books, a division of Penguin Books
USA, ISBN 0-525-65026-1)

STOPPING BY WOODS ON A SNOWY EVENING
by Robert Frost, illus. by Susan Jeffers (Dutton Children's Books, a
division of Penguin Books USA, ISBN 0-525-40115-6)

OVER THE RIVER AND THROUGH THE WOOD
by Lydia Maria Child, illus. by Iris Van Rynbach (Little, Brown and
Co., ISBN 0-316-13873-8 **pb.** Mulberry Books, an imprint of William
Morrow & Co., ISBN 0-688-11839-9)

SOPHIE AND LOU
by Petra Mathers (HarperCollins, ISBN 0-06-024071-7; **pb.**
HarperCollins Trophy, ISBN 0-06-44-3331-5 **lib.** ISBN 0-06-024072-5)

Review Books:

CORDELIA, DANCE!
by Sarah Stapler (Dial Books for Young Readers, a division of
Penguin Books USA, ISBN 0-8037-0792-4; **lib.** ISBN 0-8037-0793-2)

DANCING WITH THE INDIANS
by Angela Shelf Medearis, illus. by Samuel Byrd (Holiday House,
ISBN 0-8234-0893-0; **pb.** Holiday House, ISBN 0-8234-1023-4)

LION DANCER: ERNIE WAN'S CHINESE NEW YEAR
by Kate Waters and Madeline Slovenz-Low, photos by Martha
Cooper (Scholastic Hardcover, ISBN 0-590-43046-7; **pb.** Scholastic,
ISBN 0-590-43047-5)

SPACE CASE
by Edward Marshall, illus. by James Marshall (Dial Books for Young
Readers, a division of Penguin Books USA, ISBN 0-8037-8005-2; **pb.**

Dial Pied Piper, a division of Penguin Books USA, ISBN 0-8037-8431-7;
lib. ISBN 0-8037-8007-9)

Review Books:

ASTRONUTS: SPACE JOKES AND RIDDLES
compiled by Charles Keller, illus. by Art Cumings (Prentice-Hall
Books for Young Readers, ISBN 0-13-049909-9)

IS THERE LIFE IN OUTER SPACE?
by Franklyn M. Branley, illus. by Don Madden (HarperCollins, ISBN
0-690-04374-0; **pb.** HarperCollins Trophy, ISBN 0-06-445049-X; **lib.**
ISBN 0-690-04375-9)

LEGEND OF THE MILKY WAY
retold and illus. by Jeanne M. Lee (Henry Holt and Co., ISBN 0-8050-
0217-0)

SPORTS PAGES

by Arnold Adoff, illus. by Steve Kuzma (HarperCollins, ISBN 0-397-
32102-3; **pb.** HarperCollins Trophy, ISBN 0-06-446098-3; **lib.** ISBN 0-
397-32103-1)

Review Books:

MISS NELSON HAS A FIELD DAY
by Harry Allard and James Marshall (Houghton Mifflin Co., ISBN 0-
395-36690-9; **pb.** ISBN 0-395-48654-8)

MAKING THE TEAM
by Nancy Carlson (Carolrhoda Books, ISBN 0-87614-281-1; **pb.** Puffin
Books/Viking Penguin, a division of Penguin Books USA, ISBN 0-14-
050601-2)

SOCCER SAM
by Jean Marzollo, illus. by Blanche Sims, from the "Step Into
Reading" Series (Random House, ISBN 0-394-98406-4; **pb.** Random
House, ISBN 0-394-88406-X)

Highlighted Book

SPORTS
by Tim Hammond, photos by Dave King, an Eyewitness Book (Alfred
A. Knopf, ISBN 0-394-89616-5; **lib.** ISBN 0-394-99616-X)

STAY AWAY FROM THE JUNKYARD!

by Tricia Tusa (Macmillan Publishing Co.; **lib.** ISBN 0-02-789541-6)

Review Books:

THE SNOWY DAY
by Ezra Jack Keats (Viking Kestrel, a division of Penguin Books USA, ISBN 0-670-65400-0; **pb.** Puffin Books/Viking Penguin, a division of Penguin Books USA, ISBN 0-14-050182-7)

THE STORY OF FERDINAND
by Munro Leaf, illus. by Robert Lawson (Viking Kestrel, a division of Penguin Books USA; **pb.** Puffin Books/Viking Penguin, a division of Penguin Books USA, ISBN 0-14-050234-3; **lib.** ISBN 0-670-67424-9)

MAKE WAY FOR DUCKLINGS
by Robert McCloskey (Viking Kestrel, a division of Penguin Books USA; **pb.** Puffin Books/Viking Penguin, a division of Penguin Books USA, ISBN 0-14-050171-1; **lib.** ISBN 0-670-45149-5)

Highlighted Book:

THE VELVETEEN RABBIT
by Margery Williams, illus. by William Nicholson (Doubleday, ISBN 0-385-07725-4; **pb.** Avon Camelot, ISBN 0-385-00913-5; **lib.** ISBN 0-385-07748-3)

SUNKEN TREASURE

by Gail Gibbons (HarperCollins, ISBN 0-690-04734-7; **pb.** HarperCollins Trophy, ISBN 0-06-446097-5; **lib.** ISBN 0-690-04736-3)

Review Books:

THE TITANIC: LOST . . . AND FOUND
by Judy Donnelly, illus. by Keith Kohler, from the "Step Into Reading" Series (Random House; **pb.** ISBN 0-394-88669-0; **lib.** ISBN 0-394-98669-5)

A DAY UNDERWATER
by Deborah Kovacs (**pb.** Scholastic, ISBN 0-590-40746-5)

WHAT'S IN THE DEEP? AN UNDERWATER ADVENTURE FOR CHILDREN
by Alese and Morton Pechter (Acropolis Books, ISBN 0-87491-923-1)

TAR BEACH
by Faith Ringgold (Crown Publishers, ISBN 0-517-58030-6; **lib.** ISBN 0-517-58031-4)

Review Books:

I'M FLYING!
by Alan Wade, illus. by Petra Mathers (Alfred A. Knopf, ISBN 0-394-84510-2; **lib.** ISBN 0-394-94510-7)

ON GRANDMA'S ROOF
by Erica Silverman, illus. by Deborah Kogan Ray (Macmillan Publishing Co., ISBN 0-02-782681-3)

TO SLEEP
by James Sage, illus. by Warwick Hutton (a Margaret K. McElderry Book, an imprint of Macmillan Publishing Co., ISBN 0-689-50497-7)

THREE BY THE SEA
by Edward Marshall, illus. by James Marshall (Dial Books for Young Readers, a division of Penguin Books USA, ISBN 0-8037-8687-5; **pb.** Dial Easy-to-Read, a division of Penguin Books USA, ISBN 0-8037-8671-9)

Review Books:

FROG AND TOAD TOGETHER
by Arnold Lobel (HarperCollins, ISBN 0-06-023959-X; **pb.** HarperCollins Trophy, ISBN 0-06-444021-4; **lib.** ISBN 0-06-023960-3)

COME AWAY FROM THE WATER, SHIRLEY
by John Burningham (HarperCollins, ISBN 0-690-01360-4; **pb.** HarperCollins Trophy, ISBN 0-06-443039-1; **lib.** ISBN 0-690-01361-2)

REGARDS TO THE MAN IN THE MOON
by Ezra Jack Keats (Four Winds Press, an imprint of Macmillan Publishing Co., ISBN 0-590-07820-8; **pb.** Aladdin, an imprint of Macmillan Publishing Co., ISBN 0-689-71160-3)

THREE DAYS ON A RIVER IN A RED CANOE
by Vera B. Williams (Greenwillow Books, ISBN 0-688-80307-5; **pb.** Mulberry Books, an imprint of William Morrow & Co., ISBN 0-688-04072-1; **lib.** ISBN 0-688-84307-7)

Review Books:

ANNO'S JOURNEY
by Mitsumasa Anno (Philomel Books, ISBN 0-399-20762-7; **pb.** ISBN 0-399-20952-2; **lib.** ISBN 0-399-61165-7)

WORLDS TO EXPLORE: HANDBOOK FOR BROWNIE AND JUNIOR GIRL SCOUTS
by Girl Scouts of the U.S.A. (**pb.** ISBN 0-88441-316-0)

Mundos a Explorar
(Spanish adaption of *Worlds to Explore*; **pb.** ISBN 0-88441-331-4)

TODAY WE ARE BROTHER AND SISTER
by Arnold Adoff, illus. by Glo Coalson (Lothrop, Lee & Shepard Books, ISBN 0-688-41973-9; **lib.** ISBN 0-688-51973-3)

A THREE HAT DAY
by Laura Geringer, illus. by Arnold Lobel (HarperCollins, ISBN 0-06-021988-2; **pb.** HarperCollins Trophy, ISBN 0-06-443157-6; **lib.** ISBN 0-06-021989-0)

Review Books:

CAPS FOR SALE
by Esphyr Slobodkina (HarperCollins, ISBN 0-201-09147-X; **pb.** HarperCollins Trophy, ISBN 0-06-443143-6; **lib.** ISBN 0-06-025778-4)

MAEBELLE'S SUITCASE
by Tricia Tusa (Macmillan Publishing Co.; **lib.** ISBN 0-02-789250-6)

SHOES
by Elizabeth Winthrop, illus. by William Joyce (HarperCollins, ISBN 0-06-026591-4; **pb.** HarperCollins Trophy, ISBN 0-06-443171-1; **lib.** ISBN 0-06-026592-2)

THROUGH MOON AND STARS AND NIGHT SKIES
by Ann Turner, illus. by James Graham Hale (A Charlotte Zolotow Book, ISBN 0-06-026189-7; **pb.** HarperCollins Trophy, ISBN 0-06-443308-8; **lib.** ISBN 0-06-026190-0)

Review Books:

HORACE
by Holly Keller (Greenwillow Books, ISBN 0-688-09831-2; **lib.** ISBN 0-688-09832-0)

FATHERS, MOTHERS, SISTERS, BROTHERS: A COLLECTION OF FAMILY POEMS
by Mary Ann Hoberman, illus. by Marylin Hafner (Joy Street/Little, Brown and Co., ISBN 0-316-36736-2)

FREE TO BE . . . A FAMILY: A BOOK ABOUT ALL KINDS OF BELONGING
by Marlo Thomas and Friends (Bantam Books, ISBN 0-553-05235-7; **pb.** Bantam Books, ISBN 0-553-34559-1)

TIGHT TIMES

by Barbara Shook Hazen, illus. by Trina Schart Hyman (Viking Penguin, a division of Penguin Books USA, ISBN 0-670-71287-6; **pb.** Puffin Books/Viking Penguin, a division of Penguin Books USA, ISBN 0-14-050442-7)

Review Books:

WHEN I WAS YOUNG IN THE MOUNTAINS
by Cynthia Rylant, illus. by Diane Goode (E. P. Dutton, a division of Penguin Books USA, ISBN 0-525-42525-X; **pb.** Dutton/Unicorn, a division of Penguin Books USA, ISBN 0-525-44198-0)

PET SHOW!
by Ezra Jack Keats (Macmillan Publishing Co., ISBN 0-02-749620-1; **pb.** Aladdin, an imprint of Macmillan Publishing Co., ISBN 0-689-71159-X)

THE TERRIBLE THING THAT HAPPENED AT OUR HOUSE
by Marge Blaine, illus. by John Wallner (Four Winds Press, an imprint of Macmillan Publishing Co., ISBN 0-590-07780-5; **pb.** Scholastic, ISBN 0-590-40355-9)

TOOTH-GNASHER SUPERFLASH

by Daniel Pinkwater (Macmillan Publishing Co., ISBN 0-02-774655-0; **pb.** Aladdin, an imprint of Macmillan Publishing Co., ISBN 0-689-71407-6)

Review Books:

FILL IT UP! ALL ABOUT SERVICE STATIONS
by Gail Gibbons (HarperCollins, ISBN 0-690-04439-9; **pb.**
HarperCollins Trophy, ISBN 06-446051-7; **lib.** ISBN 0-690-04440-2)

TIN LIZZIE AND LITTLE NELL
by David Cox (The Bodley Head, ISBN 0-370-30922-7)

TRUCK SONG
by Diane Siebert, illus. by Byron Barton (HarperCollins, ISBN 0-690-04410-0; **pb.** HarperCollins Trophy, ISBN 06-443134-7; **lib.** ISBN 0-690-04411-9)

THE TORTOISE AND THE HARE
adapted and illus. by Janet Stevens (Holiday House, ISBN 0-8234-0510-9; **pb.** Holiday House, ISBN 0-8234-0564-8)

Review Books:

SAM JOHNSON AND THE BLUE RIBBON QUILT
by Lisa Campbell Ernst (Lothrop, Lee & Shepard Books, ISBN 0-688-01516-6; **pb.** Mulberry Books, an imprint of William Morrow & Co., ISBN 0-688-11505-5; **lib.** ISBN 0-688-01517-4)

HOORAY FOR SNAIL!
by John Stadler (**pb.** HarperCollins Trophy, ISBN 0-06-443075-8; **lib.** ISBN 0-690-04413-5)

ALBERT THE RUNNING BEAR'S EXERCISE BOOK
by Barbara Isenberg and Marjorie Jaffe, illus. by Diane de Groat (Clarion Books, an imprint of Houghton Mifflin Co., ISBN 0-89919-294-7; **pb.** ISBN 0-89919-318-8)

TY'S ONE-MAN BAND
by Mildred Pitts Walter, illus. by Margot Tomes (Four Winds Press, an imprint of Macmillan Publishing Co., ISBN 0-590-07580-2; **pb.** Scholastic, ISBN 0-590-40178-5; **lib.** ISBN 0-02-792300-2)

Review Books:

MAKING MUSICAL THINGS
by Ann Wiseman (Charles Scribner's Sons, ISBN 0-684-16114-1)

THE AMAZING BONE
by William Steig (Farrar, Straus & Giroux, ISBN 0-374-30248-0; **pb.** Puffin Books/Viking Penguin, a division of Penguin Books USA, ISBN 0-14-050247-5)

THE BANZA
by Diane Wolkstein, illus. by Marc Brown (Dial Books for Young Readers, a division of Penguin Books USA, ISBN 0-8037-0428-3; **pb.** Dial Pied Piper, a division of Penguin Books USA, ISBN 0-8037-0058-X; **lib.** ISBN 0-8037-0429-1)

THE WALL
by Eve Bunting, illus. by Ronald Himler (Clarion Books, an imprint of Houghton Mifflin Co., ISBN 0-395-51588-2; **pb.** ISBN 0-395-62977-2)

Review Books:

TILLIE AND THE WALL
by Leo Lionni (Alfred A. Knopf, ISBN 0-394-82155-6; **pb.** Knopf Dragonfly, ISBN 0-679-81357-8; **lib.** ISBN 0-394-92155-0)

ALL THOSE SECRETS OF THE WORLD
by Jane Yolen, illus. by Leslie Baker (Little, Brown and Co., ISBN 0-316-96891-9; **pb.** Joy Street/Little, Brown and Co., ISBN 0-316-96895-1)

MY GRANDSON LEW
by Charlotte Zolotow, illus. by William Pène du Bois (HarperCollins, ISBN 0-06-026961-8; **pb.** HarperCollins Trophy, ISBN 0-06-443066-9)

WATCH THE STARS COME OUT
by Riki Levinson, illus. by Diane Goode (E. P. Dutton, a division of Penguin Books USA, ISBN 0-525-44205-7)

Review Books:

THE LONG WAY TO A NEW LAND
by Joan Sandin (HarperCollins, ISBN 0-06-025193-X; **pb.** HarperCollins Trophy, ISBN 0-06-444100-8; **lib.** ISBN 0-06-025194-8)

MOLLY'S PILGRIM
by Barbara Cohen, illus. by Michael J. Deraney (Lothrop, Lee & Shepard Books, ISBN 0-688-02103-4; **lib.** ISBN 0-688-02104-2)

THE ISLAND OF THE SKOG

by Steven Kellogg (Dial Books for Young Readers, a division of Penguin Books USA, ISBN 0-8037-3842-0; **pb.** Dial Pied Piper, a division of Penguin Books USA, ISBN 0-8037-4122-7; **lib.** ISBN 0-8037-3840-4)

Index